Rising
with the
Morning
Star

Daily Reflections for Lent

Edited by Betty Lynn Schwab

With contributions by Gord Dunbar, Joan Farquharson, Walter Farquharson, Daniel Hansen, HyeRan Kim-Cragg, Margaret McKechney, Greer Anne Wenh-In Ng, and Anne Simmonds

Foreword by Mardi Tindal

UNITED CHURCH
PUBLISHING HOUSE

Rising with the Morning Star
Daily Reflections for Lent
Edited by Betty Lynn Schwab

Copyright © 2010
The United Church of Canada
L'Église Unie du Canada

Library and Archives Canada Cataloguing in Publication

Rising with the morning star : daily reflections for Lent / edited by Betty Lynn Schwab ; with contributions by Gord Dunbar ... [et al.] ; foreword by Mardi Tindal.

ISBN 978-1-55134-185-9

1. Lent—Prayers and devotions. 2. United Church of Canada—Prayers and devotions. 3. Devotional calendars. I. Schwab, Betty Lynn II. Dunbar, Gord

BV85.R52 2010   242'.34   C2010-905816-X

United Church Publishing House
3250 Bloor St. West, Suite 300
Toronto, ON
Canada M8X 2Y4
1-800-268-3781
www.united-church.ca/sales/ucph

MISSION AND
SERVICE FUND

UCPH is a ministry of The
United Church of Canada,
supported by the Mission and
Service Fund and readers like you.

Design: Carina Cruz Domingues, Graphics and Print
Cover photo: Dreamstime

Printed in Canada
5   4   3   2   1   14 13 12 11 10   ✠100177

CONTENTS

Week 5: Wonderful Counsellor: Healing Community

Week 6: Maker of All: Healing Creation

Holy Week: Heart of the Universe: Healing All

Foreword

You will do well to be attentive to this as to a lamp shining in a dark place, until the day dawns and the morning star rises in your hearts.

2 Peter 1:19

My spouse calls me a mystic. He knows me well and has seen how influential Christian mystics have been in my life as a follower of Christ. Guidance for daily prayer and attention to the inner life are among the many gifts of Christian mystics. "Praying with Christ," a year-long program at Five Oaks Centre that followed the spiritual exercises of St. Ignatius of Loyola, was a life-altering experience for me. Such prayer embodies a "living spirituality that sustains the journey of faith doing justice," as I remember my spiritual director saying. Books such as the one you are holding have become treasured companions in my ongoing devotional practice.

In his poem "Hagia Sophia," American Catholic mystic Thomas Merton writes, "There is in all things...a hidden wholeness."[1] He also tells us that "By the reading of Scripture I am so renewed that all nature seems renewed around me and with me. The sky seems to be a pure, a cooler blue, the trees a deeper green...the whole world is charged with the glory of God, and I feel fire and music in the earth under my feet."[2]

I feel a sense of wholeness when I read these words. Poetry and scripture take me straight to the heart of our faith and weave together my personal relationship with Christ with the prophetic call to reflect God's love for the world.

As Moderator, I have often spoken of God's abundant wholeness and healing of soul, community, and creation and of the importance of

---

1. In Thomas P. McDonnell, ed., *A Thomas Merton Reader* (New York: Image/Doubleday, 1974, 1989), p. 506.

2. Excerpt from "To the Altar of God" from *The Sign of Jonas* by Thomas Merton, copyright 1953 by The Abbey of Our Lady of Gethsemani and renewed 1981 by the Trustees of the Merton Legacy Trust, reprinted by permission of Houghton Mifflin Harcourt Publishing Company. This material may not be reproduced, stored in a retrieval system, or transmitted in any form or by any means without the prior written permission of the publisher.

participating in God's healing work. As The United Church of Canada's Song of Faith says, "In grateful response to God's abundant love, we bear in mind our integral connection to the earth and one another; we participate in God's work of healing and mending creation."

I have felt called to echo this invitation to the church to participate in God's wholeness and healing. When Betty Lynn Schwab asked how I would feel if she adopted this theme for this Lenten book, I was delighted. When I read the result, I felt overwhelmed and deeply grateful.

Greer Anne Wenh-In Ng helps us begin this Lenten journey with Christ as Hope Embodied. She unveils the wholeness in the ashes of Ash Wednesday and reminds us we are both body and spirit. She tells us that soul, community, and creation are inseparable from one another, and recalls the gift of the rabbinic tradition that would have us ask each morning, "Which part of God's world needs mending today?"

In weeks 2 and 3, Margaret McKechney and Dan Hansen guide us in our journey with Christ as Author of Life and Image of the Invisible by focusing on the healing of soul. Margaret asks how we might allow our suffering and soul-full lament to deepen our relationship with endangered species and all creatures—our sisters and brothers on this earth.

In weeks 4 and 5, Walter Farquharson and Gord Dunbar help us move deeply into healing of community, journeying with Christ as Bond of Love and Wonderful Counsellor. As Walter assures us, even in the very midst of our human desire to control, God breathes new life.

In week 6, Anne Simmonds helps us focus on the healing of creation, with Christ as Maker of All. Anne connects soul with community and creation. Day by day, we anchor ourselves in God, the Divine Healer, and enable that healing power to flow through us to the sparrows and chickadees we joyfully feed and the lilies we water so caringly.

Finally, HyeRan Kim-Cragg helps us take our last movement through Lent into Easter life, with Christ as Heart of the Universe. She, too, relies on metaphors from nature. HyeRan suggests contemplating a spider web, gently spraying water on the web, and considering how the creative tension of the web holding drops of water parallels God's beautiful web of life.

Creative tension is held in every hidden and revealed experience of wholeness—in the tension of suffering and hope, body and soul, and being both whole and in need of healing.

Rising with the Morning Star reminds me of a particular morning on a canoe trip in Algonquin Park in Ontario. As I stood on a point of land jutting into the water, I looked up to see a large, shadowy moon on one side and the bright sun rising on the other. I stood silently, held in the space between night and day. My companions were in their tents and would soon emerge. But in that precious silence at the start of the day, I contemplated shadow and light, the way things are and the way they might be, and ways that are of Christ and ways that are not.

The morning star is an ancient symbol for Christ. In Revelation 22:16, Jesus says, "I am the root and the descendant of David, the bright morning star." As we read these words together through Lent, I imagine that, like me, many of you will read and pray in the early morning during that liminal time between night and day. It is as good a time as any for praying the scriptures, receiving the gifts of these beloved writers of our United Church community, and being with Christ in stillness.

And in other times, you'll want to join companions and use this book with the excellent study guide offered by Joan Farquharson.

May these devotional practices bless your soul, your community, and God's creation. May you know the abundant wholeness of our life in Christ.

Moderator Mardi Tindal
October 2010

Week 1

Hope Embodied: Abundant Healing

Palms and Ashes

"Let me take it upon myself to speak to God, I who am but dust and ashes."

Genesis 18:27

"Sunday's palms are Wednesday's ashes." Perhaps you sang or will sing this hymn in an Ash Wednesday worship service today. It is a contemporary Lenten hymn (*Voices United* 107) that reminds Christians of the intimate connection between Jesus' triumphal entry into Jerusalem and the horror of what happened to him once he was in the city. Thus, the season of Lent begins with Ash Wednesday, using ashes from the palms of last year's Palm Sunday service.

We begin this season by setting aside time for study with our mind, reflection with our heart, and prayer for our soul's health. But the ashes remind us of our body's material connection with the earth, that we are both body *and* spirit. And genuine health needs both. This is in part why it is customary to "give up" something, such as coffee or dessert, for Lent: our bodily longing for such comforts speaks as loudly to us then as our spiritual questions do.

Another split or dichotomy typical of Western culture is that of distinguishing the individual from the community. This dichotomy differs from the understanding of the ancient Holy Land culture, the culture of the Bible. In bargaining with God for the survival of Sodom and Gomorrah, Abraham acts not so much as an individual but as part of a community and on behalf of that community. Saving the community from destruction is at stake.

In a sincere effort to bring about health in body and spirit to those who suffered much in Canada's Indian residential schools, the federal government apologized to the whole Aboriginal community and compensated individual former students, bringing some measure of release and healing for many. However, that ministry of healing souls and communities continues today. It is a vivid example of the African *ubuntu* philosophy (and theology): "I am what I am because we all are."

How can contemporary Christians overcome some of those unhealthy dualisms ("either/or") inherited by a Christianity imbued with Greek thought? One possibility lies in paying attention to wider cultural and spiritual traditions—for example, the Aboriginal Medicine Wheel with its four quadrants of the spiritual, the emotional, the physical, and the intellectual. Another is the "both...and" Taoist practice that manages to contain both the *yin* (dark/shadow, passive, cool, pliable) and the *yang* (sunny, active, warm) sides of the human self.

Might it be worth exploring the Medicine Wheel to help recover some wholeness this Lent? The Internet, the library, or a bookstore will have more information.

Prayer

God of both palms and ashes,
of hallelujahs and of tears,
we give thanks for your intention for the wholeness
of your creation and of human life.
Forgive us for the sinfulness and waywardness
that have broken this wholeness.
Teach us the way back;
show us the path of healing
in Jesus' name.
Amen.

Hymn

"Sunday's Palms Are Wednesday's Ashes" (*Voices United* 107)

Reflection Question

What is the most urgent need for healing within yourself (or your community of faith) this Lent?

Our God Who Has Created and Is Creating

*"I know that you can do all things,
and that no purpose of yours can be thwarted."*

Job 42:2

Faced with awe-inspiring natural phenomena such as earthquakes, tsunamis, and tornadoes, or with spectacular sunsets and indescribably beautiful moonrises, we may feel like Job when confronted by God's taunting "Where were you when I laid the foundation of the earth?" (Job 38:4). Realizing the limitations of our human understanding and moral imagination, we easily confess with Job, "I have uttered what I did not understand...." (Job 42:3).

As United Church people, we believe in a God "who has created and is [still] creating." How are we participating in God's creative acts in the here and now? In what ways might we ask ourselves each morning, as rabbinic tradition would have God ask, "Which part of the world needs mending?" More soberly still, in what ways need communities in the Global North ask, "How have we been violating God's creation?"

When confronted with inconvenient truths (the unsustainable exploitation of the world's natural resources, environmental degradation and climate change, unrestrained hunting of animal species to the point of extinction), most of us will probably want, with Job, to "repent in dust and ashes" (42:6).

If, as feminist theologian Sallie McFague avers, the universe is God's body, then we are summoned to do what we can to heal it. Recent efforts to practise the three Rs—reduce, reuse, recycle—to grow food more locally, and to "green" our buildings are moving toward achieving some measure of eco-justice. And, in view of the sorry history of our stewardship of the earth, one added hope lies in learning from our Aboriginal elders, sisters, and brothers in Canada and around the world so we can exist in harmony with "all our relations," even if this sometimes means finding ingenious ways to coexist with furry neighbours in our backyards!

Prayer

You have called us, ever-creating One,
to live with respect in your creation.
Teach us not only to stand in awe of your power in nature
but also to dare to partner with you
in restoring in some measure
your original design for this fragile earth,
and in sharing more equitably with all your creatures
this treasured home, both theirs and ours.
We ask for the sake of the Word, who was with you
from the beginning.
Amen.

Hymn

"Bathe Me in Your Light" (*More Voices* 82)

Reflection Questions

How have you or your group/community been partnering with God in
restoring some of creation's brokenness? What more (or new) acts would
you or your group/community like to take up, and what kind of support and
allies would you need?

ANSWERS THAT DO NOT ANSWER

Then I turned to God, to seek an answer by prayer and supplication....

Daniel 9:3

There he stands, covered in sackcloth and ashes and fasting, a civil servant successfully serving in successive empires (Babylonian, Median, Persian, Greek) far away from Jerusalem. The period predicted by the prophet Jeremiah as the duration of suffering, 70 years, is almost over. Is deliverance finally at hand? Praying on behalf of his fellow Jews in exile, Daniel seeks an answer to this urgent question. But, as the apocalyptic chapters show, the answers given him in visions must be sealed up until all has come to pass.

Prayer, so integral to the disciplines of Lent, often becomes a puzzle in the spiritual journey of Christians. Should we seek solely to be in the presence of the Divine with no other motive? Should we meditate on God's Word/ stories day and night, as Daniel does on the "books" of Jeremiah, hoping to receive some truth or wisdom? Should we only celebrate God's presence by hymns of praise and thanksgiving, or dare we, like Daniel, "seek an answer by prayer and supplication"?

Jesus describes God as a generous parent who will not give the children a stone when they ask for bread. Yet far too often followers of the Way have felt that is exactly what they have received, something they did not ask for. In such cases, how do we sustain ourselves?

Perhaps this is one of the mysteries of faith—and of life. Not every mistake we make has a chance to be rectified. Not every rift in our relationships gets repaired. Not every wrong in a community's life is righted. Not every illness is curable. Under these circumstances, we might well ask, what is healing, what is wholeness?

Let us ponder these questions this Lent.

Prayer

God of brokenness and of wholeness,
we thank you for the courage to face
what hurts and disturbs, as well as
for the times they no longer
have sway over us.
Teach us to accept the unhealable parts of ourselves:
Give us grace to live in wholeness without being healed.
In the name of the one who provoked the ultimate sacrifice,
even as he brought healing to many and to us.
Amen.

Hymn

"Spirit, Open My Heart" (*More Voices* 79)

Reflection Questions

How have you tried to deal with those parts of yourself that cannot be
healed? What has helped you live with them? What resources were you able
to draw on?

For the Healing of the Nations

God has sent me to bring good news to the oppressed,
to bind up the brokenhearted....

Isaiah 61:1

Hearing these verses from the Isaiah scroll read by Jesus at the beginning of his public ministry must have brought a surge of hope to those gathered in the synagogue at Nazareth that Sabbath, especially those who stood in need of being made whole and free. Who are they in our day? The refugees who yearn for a homeland? The violated in war, even women and children in their own homes? Are we perchance among them? It is to these who mourn to whom a garland instead of ashes is promised (61:3).

The God who declares readiness to give recompense to the exiles and their descendants is a God who loves justice (61:8)—justice not only in personal relationships but also among our communities and in our global dealings. Restorative justice means voices written out of history are brought in once again, to complete our nation's records. Distributive justice means the abundance of God's earth is shared among all. Only when such justice is done will "righteousness and praise...spring up before all the nations" (61:11). God thirsts for all justice to be accomplished.

Occasionally, grace comes in the form of invitations from violated communities in our nation that are willing to speak the truth in love and in justice. Their invitation, however, such as *Mamow Be-mo-tay-tah/ Let Us Walk Together: Racial Justice Resource 2009*[3] will also demand of us intentional acts of "decolonization" as part of that mending of relationships. Are we willing to accept such an invitation for our reconciliation and healing? And, in actively pursuing becoming an intercultural church (and world), how do we begin treating "difference" as gift in order to exercise a just hospitality, God's welcome in a world of difference?

This is the challenge—and the promise—of Isaiah 61 for our world today.

---

3. Canadian Ecumenical Anti-Racism Network, Canadian Council of Churches. Download from www.ccforum.ca/news.shtml or order from United Church Resource Distribution.

Prayer

God of exile and return,
we trust in your promise of a day of vengeance
as well as a year of your favour.
Clear our minds; open our hearts;
show us with unrelenting clarity
where we have caused oppression of others,
that we might make amends.
Teach us to stand in solidarity
with those who suffer injustice in any form,
that we might rejoice in the garland that will eventually arrive,
healing the rifts within nations and among nations
of this world you so dearly love.
Amen.

Hymn

"Jesus Christ Is Waiting" (*Voices United* 117)

Reflection Questions

In your life, your faith community's life, or the life of the world, where do you see hints of emancipation, liberation, and justice happening? How might you deepen and expand them with like-minded others?

Week 2

Author of Life: Healing Soul

YEARNING FOR THE INTRUSION OF GRACE

"Flee for your life; do not look back or stop…."

Genesis 19:17

Lot's story depicts a God of retribution bringing on the worst one can imagine, "a rain of brimstone"—apocalyptic language for a judgment on humanity. Is this really who God is? One who judges and destroys? Can we *count on* the intrusion of God's grace?

Retribution is alive and well in today's world—get tough on crime, increase the punishment, send back the immigrant now! Countless people are caught in this closed structuring of reality, where "crime and punishment" is the only view.

Consider the life of Eli. Raised in the poverty of a Canadian city, he joined a gang for protection. As guardian of younger kids in his neighbourhood, one day he sent a rival gang member out of the playground. The member's gang returned. Eli defended himself, but in the eyes of the law he was guilty. He paid for that moment of self-defence with years of his life.

Couldn't God rescue Eli as God rescued Lot? When we read the news report of all our Elis, do we not yearn for the intrusion of God's grace? How can we heal the souls of Eli and of our justice system? Or will that system just become "brimstone" for more and more Canadians?

Two awe-filled phrases frame the Lot story: "When morning dawned" and "the sun had risen on the earth." The dawning of God's grace permeates our lives like bookends on the mystery that fills the in-between. We risk allowing retributive justice to restrict our vision of the abundant grace that is this universe.

The angels allow Lot to go to Zohar because of his fears. May we be as compassionate with the fears in our own soul. The angels delay judgment until Lot is safe in Zohar. May we delay judgment until all are safe. Once Lot is safe, the sun shines not only on his horizon but also on the entire earth. The intrusion of grace in our lives can shine like that—for all.

In early 2010, astronomers were able for the first time to understand the process of birth of an enormous star known as Sharpless 2-106. Twelve thousand light-years away, with winds up to 300 kilometres per second in its core, it is literally a ring of fire. To some its destructive power is frightening. Others see a stellar nursery. What is our viewpoint—death-dealing sulphur and fire, or light and new birth?

Prayer

Creating Energy of this vast universe, you bring to birth star and wonder, tadpole and lodgepole pine. We invite your colour, energy, beauty, and awesome creativity to fill our souls with awe. Open us to the sunrise of grace. In the places bound up by impossibility, where revenge and retribution stifle the breath of life, may we be like the crocus that pushes aside the snow to bloom and awaken to new life within and among us. When the morning is dawning, may we embrace the movement of goodness in this ever-widening circle of life. Amen.

Hymns

"Live into Hope" (*Voices United* 699)
"We Cannot Own the Sunlit Sky" (*More Voices* 143)

Reflection Questions

Where do you see the possibilities for grace instead of retributive justice? How might you see a nursery where others are only fearful?

A Famine of Futures

*"I will provide for you there...so that you and your household,
and all that you have, will not come to poverty."*

Genesis 45:11

Oh, it all started so innocently, the lure of the silver, green, red, and gold
of the silk and linen. Joseph was so handsome, wouldn't the coat look
wonderful? And then there were the dreams that wended their way into
Joseph's head as he slept: sheaves bowing down and sun, moon, and stars
bending to his will. It may have been okay had he savoured his dreams in
his heart, but parading them before his brothers was what sent him on his
hair-raising journey to Egypt and captivity.

Was it in the jail, with nothing but bread to eat and cold that made his body
shiver, that Joseph suddenly understood that the dream of sheaves bowing
low was not about power and dominance? Did that insight enable him to
see that in the devastating famine—a land humbled, a people stricken—he
stood in privilege? The grandiose dreams of the sun, moon, and stars bowing
became the whispers of the universe leaning close to engage his spirit to
live in its harmony, understanding the seasons. In this lay provision for the
future. Somehow, Joseph was transformed from a proud child to one who
wept in deep sorrow at his loved ones' plight.

Do not the sun, the moon, and the stars turn to us now, in this time of grave
crisis on our beloved earth? Powerless to save this planet, they bow down
before us. Will we have the heart of compassion to listen? Can we also weep
at the devastation, the humbling of so many creatures? Does anyone have a
dream, a dream of the kind of power and zest for life that would provide for
future generations?

From coast to coast across this land, gracing the boreal forest, the woodland
caribou roam, their future seriously threatened. It takes 80 to 150 years for a
forest to grow enough lichens for caribou, their only food. They are only one
among thousands of species that are forced to bow before us as we destroy
their habitat and poison their food and the air they breathe.

Surely we must weep and lament as Joseph did, and then tenderly say as Joseph did, "I am your brother/sister. Do not fear; I will provide for you."

Prayer

From age to age, Endless Grace, you have provided for us through this good earth. In our time of famine may our souls be deepened by the cry of the blue whale, the leatherback sea turtle, and the golden eagle disappearing from the lift of the wind. Had we not become accustomed to the bright flash of the evening grosbeak, the acrobatics of the humpback whale, now crying their last breaths? Move us to tears that can express our sorrow, then enliven us with dreams of abundant healing in a world where we, as one seamless whole, can each welcome the dawn in our own way. Amen.

Hymns

"Touch the Earth Lightly" (*Voices United* 307)
"Called by Earth and Sky" (*More Voices* 135)

Reflection Questions

When did a natural disaster touch your soul? Recall your own feelings. How has healing come to that place? To your soul?

Miriam, Beloved Rebel

"Let her be shut out of the camp for seven days,
and after that she may be brought in again."

Numbers 12:14

They thought they were punishing Miriam, the rebel Yahweh loved, sending her outside the circle. Had they forgotten that it was Miriam who had run ahead into the living waters of the Reed Sea?

For Miriam knew the signs of the water, where it lay deep and where it played in the shallow sands. It would be said that when she died, the wells of the desert dried up. She'd danced to the stars, here by the Sea of Reeds (Red Sea) where the sky revealed its mystery, uninterrupted in the wide sky. The desert lark was her evening prayer, hiding so cleverly as it did among the scarce underbrush. She barely slept through the night, for that was when the desert came alive with life. As she moved in this sacred space she received as gift, her spirit came alive again, all blemishes cast by fears and jealousy dropping away.

The journey must continue, they said, but no one would move without Miriam. This Miriam of unique stature—a female prophet! But that wasn't what distinguished Miriam. It was her love of life, the joy she brought, and the songs she sang with unbridled celebration. Miriam had been condemned. She challenged the idea that God spoke only through Moses. Were not she and Aaron also able to speak the Word of the Creator? She wanted so much for them to see how the child who stood in wonder counting the falling stars also spoke clairvoyantly, how the bright sky blue of the desert lizard was a glimpse of Divine Beauty. She saw God's revealing everywhere: in the spirit of the acacia tree, in the elder who could read the shifting of the winds. How could they have missed the whisper of God in the coral reefs as they left the sea?

In the middle of the night in Bogotá, we walked through the poorest area of the city, where the recyclers lived. A little girl came dancing out into the street, holding out her arms in welcome. Others from the shadows called her

back, but she danced outside the circle and into my heart, never to
be forgotten.

PRAYER

Abundant Life, in Sabbath rest beneath the snow and alive in the spark of
human encounter, refresh our memory of your goodness. If we would tarry
in a place of despair, move deep within our being, filling the void with light,
softening the furrows of desolation with the soft rain of tenderness. Awaken
our compassion for those often sent outside the circle: homeless people,
those with mental health issues, people whose understanding of gender
differs from our own, elders living alone. May we be so filled with the love of
life in all its splendour that we too cannot help but dance outside the circle.
Amen.

HYMNS

"Teach Me, God, to Wonder" (*Voices United* 299)
"My Love Colours Outside the Lines" (*More Voices* 138)

REFLECTION QUESTIONS

Where has God been revealed to you in the last 24 hours? Where do you
really find joy? Is it not good and right that you savour it?

Of Drought and Divinity

*"[M]y God, have you brought calamity even upon the widow
with whom I am staying, by killing her son?"*

1 Kings 17:20

Do you ever play a card game where there are trump cards, the ones that
beat all the others? You always want to have one or two trump cards if
winning is your aim.

In the story about Elijah and the widow of Zarephath, Elijah plays the
trump card. The story portrays a war of ideologies, where the God of Elijah,
Yahweh, must be seen to be more powerful than Baal, the god of rain
and vegetation. To declare a long drought is essentially to proclaim Baal
dead. Other stories also prove the superiority of Elijah's God: being fed in
the wilderness by a raven; a poor widow with a son, providing for Elijah
essentially out of nothing. The climax comes when Elijah brings the widow's
son back to life: "My God brings life out of death!" is the bold proclamation.

Each carefully remembered story extols the greater power of Yahweh and
lays the groundwork for Elijah's confrontation with Baal. The final mocking
of Baal comes when Elijah calls on the name of Yahweh to light a fire, even
when the wood is soaked with water. The satire of water in the middle of
drought would not be lost on the listeners.

A church-going kid from a mixed farm on the prairies, I arrived at university
in the middle of the "death of God" movement. One day a professor brought
a wooden carving of an odd creature that was part human and part "other"
and said, "You want to see God? Here, have a look!" In the innocence
of youth, it was like a knife to my heart. The Elijah and widow story was
meant to have the same impact.

Are we still trying to prove our God is superior? Is it not ironic that the god
Elijah was proclaiming dead was the god of rain and vegetation, two things
necessary to sustain all life? What if we did not hold on to our stories as the
only sacred ones and opened ourselves to the revelations of this magnificent

universe and the gracious Creating Spirit in other ways? Is the story of Jesus walking on water really different from the sacred visions and stories of Black Elk and First Nations peoples? Each story is hallowed for the spiritual revealing it brings.

Our struggle to come to this place may be a little like Elijah's anguish in bringing life out of death. Perhaps we recognize that some things we may have believed for a lifetime are no longer alive in us. Elijah anguished at the death before him.

Even in drought, famine, and death itself, can we find what is life-giving? Is the key in the anguish? If every suicide inflicted a deep, painful wound upon our soul and the soul of each citizen, would there be anymore suicides? If the oil company anguished at the death of 1500 ducks in tailing ponds, would things be different? Despair allows full expression and can lead to healing.

Prayer

Blessed Unity, every facet of life is woven together in one seamless whole. Teach us the humility needed to recognize the sacred in places outside our ease of understanding. Where our ego might resist, may the abundant goodness stored deep in our soul stir us to wonder and move our minds to accept the considerable grace present in unexpected places. You have filled creation with light, beauty, compassion, and creative energy; open us to see its emergence. Amen.

Hymns

"Long before the Night" (*Voices United* 282)
"There Is a Time" (*More Voices* 165)

Reflection Questions

Is there something in your spiritual understanding that needs to be re-examined? When have you experienced a deep pain healed?

Turning Back the Clock

"Set your house in order, for you shall die; you shall not recover."

2 Kings 20:1

Is the pronouncement "Get your affairs in order; you have a few weeks to live" the worst life can bring? Most of us can only speculate on our response. Hezekiah weeps bitterly, but what we might expect next is decidedly absent. There is no "What did I do to deserve this?" or any litany of wrongdoings.

The meaning emerges slowly: illness never comes because God wants to punish us for our sins. Turning instead to the goodness, wholeness, and faithfulness in his life, Hezekiah hears, "I have heard your prayer, I have seen your tears; indeed I will heal you."

The sign Hezekiah asks for is curious: "the retreat of the shadow"—or we might say, "Turn back the clock." We all have times in our life when we would like the chance to redo an event or a segment of life.

When I was young, each municipality could decide whether to change the clock to daylight savings time. One year, the result was that we went to school on one time, bought groceries in another time zone, and watched the news on yet another time. Agreement only came when, each fall, we turned back the clock.

But maybe we do not need to turn back the clock. What if we believed the words of God in Isaiah 43:25, "I will not remember your sins"? Maybe there is a better way to heal than agonizing over our sins.

The miracles causing shadows to retreat are all around us. What have you fallen in love with in your wild and wonderful life on this earth? Was it the scent of the wolf willow or seaweed and salt coming like an old acquaintance? The mirth of baby coyotes proclaimed boldly to scare away the last light of day? The beauty of hand-turned wood revealing the circular secrets of ancestral wonder? The haunting memorial of old dishes from friendships deep and endearing? The orchid seed dwelling high in the atmosphere for decades, then coming to bloom on your pathway? What heart keeps still at the emotive call of the first meadowlark?

The shadows may be long and they may appear deep, but the prayers from the heart that wrought Hezekiah's miracle unfold in resounding brilliance all around us.

Prayer

Source of Wondrous Love, embracing the polar cub in the dead of winter, calling home tundra swan and monarch butterfly alike, move deeply within us to heal and comfort. Turn back any shadow cast by life's injustices and hardships, revealing an aurora of beauty and peace. As the painted turtle dares to emerge from the mud, trusting the light, providence, and goodness of earth, teach us the simplicity and wholeness of trust in you. Amen.

Hymns

"Great Is Thy Faithfulness" (*Voices United* 288)
"And When You Call for Me" (*More Voices* 96)
"Behold, Behold, I Make All Things New" (MV 115)

Reflection Question

What is it about the movement in a symphony, the embrace of a friend, or the splendour of a sunset that helps us experience healing?

To You, O God, I Call

I lift up my hands toward your most holy sanctuary.

Psalm 28:2

Psalm 28 evoked this prayer from the heart:

From the depth of my being, I call to you, Blessed Energy of this expansive cosmos. If I open my spirit to your magnificence, should my mind try to encompass the awe that is your being? If I touched even some of the mystery, I would be forever changed. If you were to echo back only silence, the despair of my soul would be beyond comprehension.

How do I know that among the billions of sentient beings on this earth you would hear my voice? So I cry from the depths for help. I lift my hands to the forest filled with song, the marshland wombs of earth, the sustaining rocks, the ocean deep, and the fertile soil: your most holy sanctuary. Hear my voice, Blessed Unity, that I might know the blossoming of your grace.

Blessed be the keeper of the bluefin tuna, the fingers that blend the harp's notes into the day, the tiller of soil, the weaver of cloth, the sugar workers, dreamers, and wise ones. Blessed be the stars, the night heron, the shy badger, and the reluctant rose. For all have heard my pleadings—we are one seamless whole.

How do I name that which is my strength and shield? Is it this atmosphere—fine gossamer thread that surrounds this earth? Or perhaps my shield is the passion for justice that protects the soul from the icy destruction of discrimination, poverty, and hunger.

Yet surely love itself protects me like no other. Only in its gentle and daring embrace can I plummet the depths of my own soul.

When I trust my heart in all these matters, then I know and I am helped. The deep wisdom of all that is can surely fill my soul to overflowing. And I sing with the ripple of the grasses, the crowd marching to freedom, the voice of compassion, the soft colours of the underside of the leaf, water that quenches, and music that restores. I give thanks. I give thanks.

Hymn

"Open My Eyes, That I May See" (*Voices United* 371)
"You, Creator God, Have Searched Me" (*More Voices* 131)

Reflection Questions

When have you known the presence of Divine Grace? What calls forth in your soul the awe and wonder of Holy Mystery?

Listen, Listen, Listen Carefully!

Incline your ear, and come to me; listen, so that you may live.

Isaiah 55:3

They wanted to dance all night to the beat of the *bodu beru* (the big drum), Baya and her granddaughter Amishka, but here in the Maldives it was December, monsoon season. So they huddled together in the hut, and Baya told stories of her youth: of warm days under the banyan tree, bodysurfing far out into the warm kiss of the waves. Amishka always said, "Grandma, when I grow up I will name my baby Baya so she can be just like you!"

Hundreds of miles away the most powerful nations gathered around a table, Amishka's dreams in the palms of their hands. It was the Copenhagen Climate Change Conference, where the future of the planet—and how much the sea would rise—was being decided. It seemed that they alone could mediate life itself. Had they listened to Amishka? Had they hard the Maldives' cries to save their nation from the rising sea?

Until Isaiah's time it was thought that only monarchy mediated the eternal covenant of love and life. Throwing aside this thinking, Isaiah declares, means that there are no barriers. To the goodness, beauty, justice, and bounty that is life in the presence of all that is sacred, all are invited. Come! The invitation, like the breath of life, is without price. Surely we will not turn away for better company. But we must be the ones who listen, listen, listen carefully.

Listen, listen, listen carefully—for the voice of reverence, the whisper of grace, the unexpected footsteps of holiness are as soft as the footfall of the firefly and as strong as the tensile thread of a spider's web.

I had to still myself to hear it—the tinkle. It was the first ice freezing on the pond. I did not know that frost makes music.

Did you read the invitation in the tatting of the hoar frost framed in turquoise light? Did you hear it in the lily's unfolding, the ring of the builder's hammer? Will you resist the enticement to gather sorrow, delight, and meaning in life's basket like a midsummer gardener's harvest? As we absorb the smell of molten honey, fresh grief, old hats and spices, sage and worn skates, we savour their worth. Listen to the ache of heart's compassion searching for justice. Even in times of deep despair, no one is without an invitation.

Steeped in Andean thought, the People's World Conference on Climate Change and Mother Earth's Rights was a response to what people heard at Copenhagen. The People's Conference used terms like "living well" to describe a way of life that seeks not to live "better" at the cost of others and nature but to live in harmony with all. These people seek a Universal Declaration of the Rights of Mother Earth and dream of it enshrined in every constitution worldwide. They listen to Amishka's dreams and to the Maldives' cry. They give possibility to the dreams of Amishka. Listen, listen, listen carefully!

Prayer

With amazement, Glorious Unity, we recognize that we hold the cusp of life in our hands. You have given us a sacred trust of mountain and plain, marsh and desert, centipede, whale, nuthatch, and human, whose destinies are inextricably linked. May we mediate life in all its fullness and invite all beings to an everlasting banquet of life. Amen.

Hymns

"All Things Bright and Beautiful" (*Voices United* 291)
"Like a Healing Stream" (*More Voices* 144)

Reflection Questions

Recall a time when you felt fully alive. What does it mean to embrace life in all its fullness? Often meaning must be sought. What gives your life meaning?

Week 3

Image of the Invisible: Healing Soul

Resiliency and More

Jesus rebuked him, saying, "Be silent, and come out of him!"
When the demon had thrown him down before them, he came out
of him without having done him any harm.

Luke 4:35

Sometimes when you are in the midst of a challenging situation, you feel as if there is no way out. Everything seems to be falling in on you. You wonder what to do and how you will ever manage. You may even ask, "Where is God in all of this? Why isn't God helping me?"

As a parent I sometimes feel this way. When I have had a long day at home with my young boys, I feel exhausted. They try my patience, and they want me to play with them constantly. Being an older father in mid-life, I may have wisdom—but I do not have the energy of a 20- or 30-year-old! After that, moving into my pastoral role as a minister for an evening church meeting takes a little time. But once I get into the car, begin the drive, and take a few deep breaths, something happens, and I settle anew into an awareness of God's embracing presence.

It is a challenge to realize that God is active even in what we perceive as challenging moments. Another challenge is realizing that we cannot free or heal ourselves—that we have to let God draw us into new life. The lure of God is always toward healing and new life.

In painful ways, we may know what it is like to be possessed, taken over by some negative life-situation or desire. Perhaps we have forgotten the power of the Holy Spirit leading us. Perhaps we need to be called out of ourselves to be our fullest selves. When we let Jesus Christ call us forth, firmly addressing our challenges, we often find that we are not as badly off as we originally thought. We might also find that what we previously thought we needed or depended on is not necessarily so. Often this process of discernment can take time, but everything can also change in the twinkling of an eye.

That is the nature of the baptismal life and the ongoing call of Jesus. In our baptism, we turn from an old way of life to a new one. We keep doing that throughout our faith journey—coming back to God.

These 40 days of Lent are about being open to a deeper relationship with God. When we call out in faith to God, letting God see our whole selves— even our most challenging, negative, and uncomfortable aspects—we have an opportunity to be cleansed and made new. In our resiliency, we find that we are filled with new energy. We are also more ready to help God in bringing about abundant healing to others. The healing call of Jesus' presence restores our soul—our relationship with God. It brings us back to who we are created to be, and helps us to be ready for something new.

Prayer

Gracious God,
hearer of all cries,
listen to us when we call out to you,
even when the demons inside us
seem to know you better than we do.
Open us to the healing of our souls that only you can provide,
that we might come to our fullest selves,
be who we really are as your followers,
and be ready for something unexpected and new.
We pray in the name of the One who can speak to the depths of our hearts,
and make us ready for such an adventure, Jesus Christ.
Amen.

Hymns

"Silence, Frenzied, Unclean Spirit" (*Voices United* 620)
"In You There Is a Refuge" (*More Voices* 84)

Prayer-in-Action

Write out the gospel story in Luke 4:31–35 and put it in your pocket, wallet, or purse. Let the Word of God enter your heart and be a part of each waking moment. Pray for God to give you something in particular from this reading. Stay with that. Expect God to respond. Wait.

LIVING FAITH

"I say to you, stand up and take your bed and go to your home."
Immediately he stood up before them....

Luke 5:24–25

A man who is unable to move physically is empowered by the call of Jesus to get up and go home. He is enabled to do what he thought he could not. The faith-filled people surrounding him are amazed, including the scribes and the Pharisees, who can be the most critical.

In biblical times, sickness was considered a result of sin and led to a person's being judged unclean and cut off from the community. Though many know better today, we are often challenged to make daily life-decisions that contribute to our health and wholeness. That is never easy.

When we lose sight of God's presence in and around us, we often choose to move in directions that may not be the best for our body, mind, and spirit. But as Jesus calls us from our life-situations, especially our paralysis, and asks us to take on a new perspective and orientation, from what seems like an ending comes a new beginning.

A few years ago, I awoke one Saturday morning just before Christmas to find that I could not move the right side of my face, not even my eye and mouth. I couldn't blink or smile. As I looked in the mirror to shave, I was devastated. My older son, who was nearby, saw my tears.

For the first time in my life I had to call in sick and couldn't lead the last service of the season of Advent. It was to focus on how God comes into our lives in unexpected ways. I didn't know what my future would hold in terms of healing—full, partial, or not at all—and how long it would take. The eventual diagnosis was Bell's palsy.

Throughout it all, however, I continued to faithfully do my church ministry and attend to my family. I rested when able and did only what I needed, being selective about any extra activities. After some years of treatment and patience, I was cured.

Over the years, I have learned through experience and openness to the Spirit how God is working out God's purposes of healing and wholeness with humanity. As with the story of the paralyzed man, so it is with us. Whatever position we have or hold on to in life, Jesus calls us to arise and get on our way. As we receive and follow his words, we will know God's way.

Prayer

Gracious God,
forgiver of all waywardness,
listen to us when we call out to you,
especially when we are unable to move.
Open us to the healing of our souls
that only you can provide.
Help us confess our forgetfulness of you and receive your forgiveness.
Raise us up to new life!
We pray in the name of the One
who goes beyond all human thought and imagination,
brings us back to God,
and draws us into new intimacy, Jesus Christ.
Amen.

Hymns

"In All Our Grief and Fear" (*Voices United* 609)
"Are You a Shepherd?" (*More Voices* 126)

Prayer-in-Action

Write out the gospel lesson in Luke 5:17–26 and put it in a handy place. Read it slowly several times during your day. Ponder it. Let the Word of God enter your heart and be a part of each moment. Pray for God to give you something in particular from this reading. Think about how you might be lifted up out of your place and life into something new, and what that would entail. Let God's Word bring this out of you!

Faith Makes Well

She came up behind him and touched the fringe of his clothes,
and immediately her hemorrhage stopped.

Luke 8:44

My old chocolate Labrador retriever, Gabe, my dog since I was first
ordained, was consistently bleeding from his mouth. As well, his breath was
terrible.

So, in fear and trepidation, I looked into his mouth, only to find a growth
the size of a golf ball. A visit to the veterinarian confirmed the inevitable—
that Gabe had cancer and would at best be able to live somewhat
comfortably for another few weeks if medicated. That would give us some
time to say goodbye.

Would my faith make him well? I certainly thought I had some and had
worked intentionally at it for years. Deep down, however, I knew the illness
would soon take its course, and we would have to put Gabe down fairly
soon.

Why didn't my faith make him well? That is a question many of us ask
at times of suffering and death. If I could have taken Gabe to Jesus and
touched his clothes, would that have worked?

In the gospel story, an ill woman goes into the crowd, finds Jesus, and
touches him—a man. Both no-no's for a sick woman. She shouldn't be in
public, and she shouldn't be touching a man.

Deep down, this woman of faith knows who Jesus is and will go to any
length to make sure she gets close to him. In fact, she puts her own life on
the line to do that.

The ongoing call for disciples is to keep turning to Jesus, and through faith
and the work of the Holy Spirit, expect the unforeseeable. It is a call for
openness to and relationship with Christ. What others think of us does not
really matter; what does matter is how we let Jesus lead us.

The physical outcome is very important to us. However, an intentional encounter with Jesus is an encounter that will bring about healing of the soul—a deep inner sense of renewal and relationship with the Holy. Only God determines what that will actually be in the end.

PRAYER

Gracious God,
One in touch with all,
receive our call in need,
even when our life is crowded and it is difficult to get to you.
Open us to receive the abundant healing of our souls
that only you can provide.
Then may we continue to seek you out boldly
and come close to you,
even knowing the odds and what others might think.
In letting you become close to us,
we courageously risk being your followers
and living in your Holy Presence.
We pray in the name of the One
whose power goes out to all who seek him
and brings them new life, Jesus Christ.
Amen.

HYMNS

"Draw Us in the Spirit's Tether" (*Voices United* 479)
"Love Is the Touch" (*More Voices* 89)

PRAYER-IN-ACTION

Write out the gospel story in Luke 8:42b–48 and carry it with you. When rereading it throughout the day, let God bring you to a new sense of meaning. Listen to your thoughts and feelings, even what you don't like about the text or find problematic. Be open to anything, even the completely unexpected. Let God lead you.

Thankful Faith

*[O]ne of them, when he saw that he was healed, turned back, praising God
with a loud voice.... Then Jesus asked, "Were not ten made clean?
But the other nine, where are they?"*

Luke 17:15, 17

Current Christian practice sometimes shows that when we are well and
things are going along smoothly, we feel less need for God. However, when
life takes a turn for the worse, we often start praying a lot more. We want
God on our side.

Somehow we think that if we can only pray a little harder and more
frequently, God will hear us and do what we want. We may even begin to
believe that faith is something we can create or control: with more prayers
comes more faith. Or we may think we deserve something by being who we
are.

Having completed an interim ministry appointment and not subsequently
finding another position, I had some time to think and to be with God..
I gained a new sense of what God has done in my life and how God has
blessed me. There were some aspects of my life that I needed to attend to,
some things that had been set aside for many years.

Now I had the time to begin to work at these again, and to birth new ideas
and perspectives, even a deeper sense of self and of vocation. I had not
planned it that way, but I perceived that God was bringing me healing. The
old way was out; a new way was coming in. I learned that I had to make
more room for God, letting certain things go.

Being thankful to God is at the heart of such learning. While choosing to
let God be the energy of your life is the central movement, thanksgiving
and praise open us to this movement, deepening our relationship with God.
God not only brings us gifts and blessings but also the sheer gift of each day
of life. There is something utterly spectacular about the ordinary that makes
it truly holy!

Where are these holy moments for you? How is God working in you today? How are you returning to the altar of God in thanks and praise?

Radical thankfulness is content with what already is and whatever has been given to us. You realize what God has done and is doing. You can do nothing but thank and praise God. Radical thankfulness has no desire for more or for something better, as with a consumer mentality. There is satisfaction with what is and deep recognition that what is is an immense blessing, revealing afresh the goodness and love of God. More importantly, radical thankfulness evokes the desire to work with God and reveals how we can do that work, sustaining God's creation through relationships of health and wholeness. Thanks be to God!

Prayer

Gracious God,
Giver of All Life,
forgive us when we forget to return to you
and give you thanks.
Help us experience the depths of gratitude.
Help us receive abundant healing of our souls.
Help us savour the depths of life possible only as your disciples.
We pray in the name of the One who gave completely,
in humble service to you,
Jesus Christ.
Amen.

Hymns

"At the Name of Jesus" (*Voices United* 335)
"Spirit, Open My Heart" (*More Voices* 79)

Prayer-in-Action

Write out the gospel story in Luke 17:11–19 and carry it with you, but make an extra copy you can pass on to someone else. As a mid-week sharing opportunity, tell that person what you are doing and invite him or her to take the reading and meditate on it. Be bold. Take a risk. Be open to the completely unexpected as God's Word continues to grow and become in you.

Blind Faith

He said, "Lord, let me see again." Jesus said to him,
"Receive your sight; your faith has saved you."

Luke 18:41–42

My friend Peggy is blind. Now in her 80s, I met her while I was at university. She sang in the church choir where I had just started as organist. When she found out where I lived, she asked if I would mind driving her home after rehearsal. Over time, we became great friends.

A dream Peggy had was to go to the Metropolitan Opera in New York City. So one day I took her on the train. She had the time of her life, complete with a horse and carriage ride in Central Park and a meal in the restaurant overlooking the skating rink at Rockefeller Center.

Though my words helped her see what was there, what she had never seen before, Peggy taught me how to see what is not so obvious.

Peggy had a tough life, which she referred to in her unpublished biography as "no bed of roses." Not inhibited by her physical blindness, however, she was there for me when I had a tough time. Along with her housemate and caregiver Eleanor, who is now in her late 90s, they often provided hospitality comparable to no other. Good times together led to opportunities to share our life stories, offer mutual support, and gain new insights into ourselves, the church, and God's world.

Clearly, the blind beggar knows Jesus can fulfill his request to see again. And he is persistent about being heard by Jesus. For good reasons, mostly religious, the disciples hold back this potential relationship until Jesus says something and tells them what to do. Finally, the demanding man is brought to Jesus.

Though the man is able to see again, what is unique about this story is that he is not sent on his way but instead chooses to stay and follow Jesus. Healing comes to us when we let God be with us and energize us, bringing us to a new sense of the "who" and "what" of our lives and our community.

Such spiritual discernment is not seen through the human eye, which cannot always see what really needs to be felt and experienced. God does this work within us, drawing us into something new.

Prayer

Gracious God,
who stops to attend to all calling out,
be present to us as we talk together.
Listen to us when we seek your direction.
Open us to your abundant healing
that only you can provide,
so we can see your Way more clearly.
We pray in the name of the One who listens intently
and invites all to walk with him,
whole and made new.
Amen.

Hymns

"Hail to God's Own Anointed" (*Voices United* 30)
"What Calls Me from the Death" (*More Voices* 93)

Prayer-in-Action

What did you learn from your sharing yesterday? Were you able to do it? If so, what was that like? If not, what stopped you? Pay attention to the details. Maybe there is something you were previously blind to regarding your faith, but now you see it. Maybe the something is yet to be seen!

Striking Faith

Then one of them struck the slave of the high priest and cut off his right ear. But Jesus said, "No more of this!" And he touched his ear and healed him.

Luke 22:50–51

For whatever reason, we sometimes cut off our relationships with certain people. It might be because of something colleagues have said or done. Likewise, relationships with friends and even family can become too troubled. No one is insulated from this reality.

If we were not Christian, it might be easier to let go of people, ignoring or denying the problem. But the call of the gospel always encourages us to look closely at our self and our relationships, including our relationship with God and Jesus Christ. Christ's calling is to a life marked by important qualities: love, forgiveness, reconciliation, and lasting, deep healing.

Before today's text, the apostles had just eaten the Passover meal with Jesus. After speaking about the events soon to unfold, he said that if they didn't have a sword, they should buy one. Hearing there were already two swords among them, he decided two were enough; then they all went to the garden, where Judas came with the crowd.

We can easily imagine that intense moment: the apostles are exhausted, confused, and afraid. The soldiers are not in a jovial mood. Judas is awash in guilt or wondering if he is doing the right thing. Anxiety is everywhere.

A voice rings out: "Jesus, should we strike with the sword?" Before Jesus can answer, a sword flashes in the night. The slave screams. Blood flows down the cheek and garment. Jesus' voice is firm: "No more of this!"

Fortunately, our relationships are not nearly as dire as this moment! Yet there is always a strong connection between personal growth and growth as a disciple in Christ. When we let ourselves be nurtured by the Spirit, there is genuine opportunity for God to move us beyond our anger and hurt. The dead end we think has no way out can be radically changed. This is no easy road: God's Way requires diligence and perseverance and sometimes gets messy before the new direction is discerned. We may not have all the answers right away, but we do have a strong sense of being embraced in God's loving care.

Human response to fear and hurt is too often physical and emotional violence. Jesus' response is to heal. Working deeply with our faith and faith community, we too heal our self, our relationships, and our beloved world.

Prayer

Gracious God,
who has the ability to make sense of our messy state,
listen to us when we feel cut off or cut out,
when the pressure of worldly life
makes us act in unkind ways,
even dropping relationships.
Open us to your abundant healing
that only you can provide,
that we might come to see
how we cut ourselves off from you.
May we know deeply that you are always present,
urging us into a life of repentance, forgiveness, and reconciliation.
We pray in the name of the wounded healer, Jesus Christ.
Amen.

Hymns

"As the Deer Pants for the Water" (*Voices United* p. 766)
"Love Knocks and Waits" (*More Voices* 94)

Prayer-in-Action

Think back to yesterday. When might you have used a more healing, reconciling approach to people you encountered? As a disciple of Christ and a healer yourself, how might you act in new ways from this day forward? Make note of these ways and where there is any challenge in this for you.

OpeNiNg FaitH

They brought to him a deaf man who had an impediment in his speech…. [Jesus]
took him aside in private…put his fingers into his ears, and he spat and touched his
tongue…. And immediately his ears were opened, his tongue was released,
and he spoke plainly.

Mark 7:32–33, 35

A little privacy, fingers in ears, spittle, and a touch of the tongue, as well
as a brief prayer—that is all it takes for Jesus to open this man's ears and
release his tongue.

In a discussion of a similar story during a worship service, a congregant
once asked, "Did Jesus really do that?" Though I responded quickly and
affirmatively with a "yes," I wondered later (the next minute, actually) if I
had really heard what she was asking about her own life. Maybe if I hadn't
opened my mouth so soon I would have encouraged more conversation, and
a deeper part of her soul-searching would have emerged.

In the next verse (Mk. 7:36), Jesus says to the people something like
this: "Please keep this to yourselves. There is much more that you must
experience and understand about this gospel of God that I am living out
and proclaiming before you tell everyone about it. For now, contain the
excitement and be ready to hear more."

As with those in the story who are told not to tell anyone, we can short-
circuit the person and presence of God. We can make God out to be who
we want God to be, and we do the same with Jesus. Or, the glamour of a
miracle can overpower the truth that needs to be heard and seen, which
concerns Jesus far more. We often see this happening with the first disciples.
Like the apostles, we can get caught in our perceptions and emotions and
easily jump to conclusions. A process of discernment is required.

Deep, internal healing is about discerning God head-on through Jesus
Christ and the ministry of the Holy Spirit. It is about getting personal
with Jesus, perhaps through a spiritual guide, and letting Christ become
personal with us and touch us. As we do so, he draws us out of ourselves into

something new. But discerning intimacy with God is essential, listening for God as *the* energy and shaper of our life, and learning to see more clearly the fullness of God at work transforming in us and in all. Then we can experience the multi-dimensional, ever-pervasive, luring love-call of God even more. We are unleashed to know greater freedom and new life.

At communion, the bread is broken so it can be shared. We don't just stare at a lovely, fresh-baked loaf. As we are intentional about the healing of our own soul, opening ourselves to God's grace, we learn how to be with others. We are able to invite them to explore God's healing power already working in them, bringing them to new life.

PRAYER

Gracious God,
Hearer of the Unimaginable,
silence us when we only want to listen to ourselves,
when our tongues are flapping so fast,
and our lives are filled to the brim with activities.
Open us to your abundant healing,
that we might slow down,
turn again and again to face you, and receive your new life.
We pray in the name of the One
who takes us beyond our imagination, Jesus Christ.
Amen.

HYMNS

"When Seed Falls on Good Soil" (*Voices United* 503)
"Three Things I Promise" (*More Voices* 176)

PRAYER-iN-ACTiON

Sit quietly in a private and comfortable place, and receive the culmination of your weekly prayer and scripture life. As a new Sunday emerges tonight, await God's personal Word of new life to you. Wait in expectation of what God has done, is doing, and will yet do in Christ Jesus through the Holy Spirit. Be at peace, and know that God is with you, all is well, and God is working in your life and bringing abundant healing to your soul.

WEEK 4

Bond of Love: Healing Community

The Gift of Diversity

God confused the language of all the earth....

Genesis 11:9

The story in Genesis 11:1–9 carries a powerful message for our world, a world that is in many ways shrinking.

It speaks of a people building the Tower of Babel, which becomes the Tower of Babble. The builders are powerful and wealthy. They can exert power over all their neighbours and enforce an amazing uniformity of thought and practice. They have one language and they intend that, as their influence spreads and deepens, soon the whole world will have but one language, making communication easy.

The story of Pentecost told in the Book of Acts is often considered the reversal of Babel. By the action of the Spirit, people understand the disciples despite the many languages they speak. Barriers of language and culture are overcome, and an amazing unity is created.

This Pentecostal unity is one that flourishes within diversity, a unity enriched by difference. Even ecologically speaking, diversity is essential. We have only recently begun to understand that the disappearance of species threatens the health of the natural communities all our human communities depend on.

Our world has been cursed by human attempts to impose an unholy conformity upon everyone in a society. Conformity has been imposed by empire after empire. Conforming societies have welcomed rule by an elite few or accepted the tyranny of cruel and maniacal dictators. Such societies have frequently demanded loyalty to political, economic, or religious dogmas and have too often stifled movements nurturing freedom and creativity. Generally, conforming societies are cynical about human nature and look down on all who are categorized as the unwashed, the unsaved, the ignorant, the uncivilized, or the savage. The drive to conformity manifests itself in powerful nation-states and economic empires but also in small communities, cults, and denominations that see the "way we've always done it" as the only way, the right way, and the way blessed by God.

Into the very midst of this human desire to control, God breathes new life. Stones are rolled away from tombs of convention and control. In valley after valley of dry bones there is a stirring, a moving, a coming together, and a dancing in a unity created by a free and freeing Spirit that is excitingly new and life-giving.

PRAYER

Holy One, help us see the places where we would seek to impose an uncompromising conformity in our families, our congregations, and our communities. Let us see where we have closed doors on others and on new and challenging ideas. Help us celebrate diversity as a gift offered us and as a source of new life for our church and your world. Amen.

HYMNS

"Bring Many Names" (*Voices United* 268)
"When I Needed a Neighbour" (VU 600)
"To Us All, to Every Nation" (VU 694)

PRAYER-IN-ACTION

List times when you have felt stifled by an enforced conformity. Think of someone whose approach to life is very different from your own. Invite that person to share with you her or his understandings and perspectives.

You Are Entering a Slavery-Free Zone

"I will free you…and deliver you from slavery…."

Exodus 6:6

Slavery and oppression in any form stand in direct opposition to healthy and healing communities.

There are slaveries we endure and slaveries we accept as just the way things are and always have been. There are even slaveries we welcome, sometimes because they carry with them some peculiar advantage for us and sometimes because we cannot imagine life apart from them. This is a theme I have often heard spoken of in gatherings of Alcoholics Anonymous and similar groups. It is a cry I have heard voiced by people struggling with abuse or oppressive family relationships. It is essential, too, that we name those slaveries and burdens imposed in the name of God—and those overlooked or even blessed in the name of God.

An essential part of our journey toward health in community is naming the slaveries we have experienced—sometimes as those who were enslaved and sometimes as those who, deliberately or not, held others in a form of slavery.

As we read history—the history of almost any people, even the history of the people of the Bible—we are shocked by the acceptance of slavery. Yet we know that the key story of the Book of Exodus, and indeed the whole of the Hebrew history as recorded in scripture, is an elaboration based on the story of God's freeing an enslaved people and the formation of a new people called to explore and live a new ethic of justice, mercy, and peace.

The health we seek within community calls us to name the slaveries and oppressions that thrive around us and sometimes entrap us. That same call to health invites us to believe that all slaveries can by thrown off. We are not condemned to repeat the excesses and evils of yesterday or of another century.

Jesus overturns the tables of the money-changers in the temple, condemning the unnecessary burdens they have placed on ordinary people. In doing so he invokes the memory of Jeremiah (chapter 7), who thunders against a people who oppress one another, commit evil upon evil, and then hide sanctimoniously behind the façade of worship and temple observance.

There is no place for slavery or for imposing burdens on others in the ethic of a people called to embody and practise God's justice, healing, and love.

Prayer

Empower your people, O God, to follow in the Way of Jesus. Empower your people to name the things that enslave them or others. Empower them to recognize and fight against the things that lay burdens on brothers and sisters. Empower your people to live each day with a fiery passion for justice and health for all. Amen.

Hymns

"We Are Marching" (*Voices United* 646)
"Make Me a Channel of Your Peace" (VU 684)
"Though Ancient Walls" (VU 691)

Prayer-in-Action

Recall an occasion when you, or someone very close to you, experienced a form of slavery. Think about the people and circumstances that helped as the slavery was named and moved away from. Where might you be called to act as an agent of freedom and liberation?

I Need Three Volunteers: You, You, and You

All those who were enrolled…qualified to do the work of service….

Numbers 4:46–47

The entire book of Numbers reminds us that the journey from slavery to a new beginning for the Hebrew people was a journey fraught with hardship and difficulty. Many times the people complained bitterly and, feeling lost, were ready to abandon the enterprise. God's patience got a good workout during the years of wandering and hiding out in the wilderness, but God had no intention of abandoning the people.

Moses received instructions to take a census of the people. The identification of "everyone able to go to war" was no more than a restating of "every male…from twenty years old and upward" (Num. 1:2–3). The census identified adult males according to household and family lineage, a totally patriarchal scene.

Probably many who read Numbers 1–4 wonder how this account is relevant to their faith journey. Two things stand out and transcend the limitations of history and culture. First, for community to survive and come to a place of health, all who are able must carry responsibility for the community. Each person must play a part in assuring the welfare of the community and of every individual member of the community. Second, the Israelites had to know that the major symbol of their community's journey in the name of their liberating God was the ark of the covenant. The presence and protection of the ark was the glue that held them together in community. What is the glue for our faith community today?

Most of us are members of several communities at any given moment of our lives. We live in geographic and political communities. We live in faith communities. We live in families and volunteer groups and associations. We know communities in our workplaces and where we gather for recreation and renewal. Sometimes it is hard to balance our commitments in these varied communities.

Community—healthy community—is intentional. It requires organization, formal and informal, that defines the areas of responsibility carried by all and also by each community member. Any community we are part of is either being built and renewed, or it finds itself in a state of disorganization and disintegration. Community is defined by purpose and maintained by each member consciously choosing that which brings life to the community and sets it upon new paths of service.

PRAYER

God, you call us into communities that define us, and you call us into places of service. Let your Spirit guide us into renewed commitment that seeks life and health for all around us. Broaden our scope of vision so we see your hand at work around us, and so our hands and hearts do the work to which you daily call us. Amen.

HYMNS

"Jesus Calls Us" (*Voices United* 562)
"Jesus, You Have Come to the Lakeshore" (VU 563)
"Jesus' Hands Were Kind Hands" (VU 570)
"Jesus Came, a Child like Me" (VU 583)

PRAYER-IN-ACTION

Identify a new sphere of service that the Spirit of God is calling you to give attention to. Prayerfully consider how that is likely to take shape in the days ahead.

Some Days I'd Rather Play My Harp

*So all the elders of Israel came to the king at Hebron; and King David made
a covenant with them at Hebron before God, and they anointed David
king over Israel.*

2 Samuel 5:3

The tribes gather. They need a leader, a king. David has already been
providing the leadership they need, so his abilities are known to them. The
tribes are convinced that God has chosen David for the role of leader of the
people. A covenant is made, and the parties to it are David, the people, and
God.

We seem to have a hard time understanding leadership at this time in our
history as nation and as church. The distrust of leaders and leadership seems
endemic. We know that many in positions of leadership have abused the
trust given them. We know that power tends to corrupt, and we have often
been reminded of the saying that "absolute power corrupts absolutely."

Sometimes power is exerted openly in good ways and in bad. Sometimes
it is hidden and becomes even more dangerous. The critics of power and
the powerful are themselves exercising power, and again this can help
community or destroy it.

Good leaders know their role must be a leadership of service. They
also know the temptations of power and the potential to use power for
destructive purposes. Good leaders can never be cynical about the people
they lead and that they cannot cease to love and respect the communities in
which they exercise power and influence.

Perhaps the key to good leadership lies in covenant, in the awareness of
responsibilities accepted and purposes shared.

When God is a signatory to covenants of leadership, certain realities are always present. All power is limited, and leaders must accept with joy and relief the reality of that limitation. All positions of power are held accountable to the people, to the people's story, to the future, and ultimately to the health of the whole creation. Power is consultative, and leaders know and use the tools of self-reflection and spiritual discernment.

Effective leadership shares in the creative and healing powers of God. It lives not for itself or for the benefit of those temporarily called to exercise leadership, but rather for the sake of community that seeks to be both healthy and health-giving. We see in Jesus' work and hear in Jesus' words that which we can identify as God-given and God-blessed leadership. "I have set you an example," he tells his disciples (Jn. 13:15).

Prayer

Often we have prayed, "For thine is the kingdom." Help us, gracious God, to reflect on this simple phrase. Help us to know that when the kingdom is yours it cannot be claimed by any of us. Hear our prayers for all who exercise leadership and authority in our governments and institutions, in our councils and congregations. Help us know when and where we are called to exercise or share tasks of leadership. Help us to understand the significance of Jesus kneeling to wash the feet of reluctant and protesting disciples. Amen.

Hymns

"Today We All Are Called to Be Disciples" (*Voices United* 507)
"We Have This Ministry" (VU 510)
"O God of All the Many Lands" (VU 523)
"Let There Be Light" (VU 679)

Prayer-in-Action

List three or four people who exercise leadership today. In what ways do you see reflected the kind of leadership Jesus exercised? Which world leaders of today do you believe will have the greatest impact on the shape of our global society?

HUMANS ARE HARSHER

"I am in great distress; let me fall into the hand of God, for God's mercy is very great; but let me not fall into human hands."

1 Chronicles 21:13

Even the best rulers make foolish choices. The most virtuous can fall flat on their faces and stand judged and condemned. A life of service can be thrown into question by one stupid or inappropriate word or deed. Our world seems hungry for scandal and willing to pass on rumour and innuendo without so much as a "maybe we should check this out."

In the reading today we have to smile as David says, "Let me fall into the hand of God, for God's mercy is very great; but let me not fall into human hands." Would you not think that we who make so many mistakes, we who so often choose paths that lead to destroying ourselves and others, would have some understanding and greater room in our hearts for forgiveness and grace? No. It doesn't work that way. Like David, if we know the story, we'll take our chances with God and God's mercy rather than face the judgment of our peers.

Thinking about David's choice may remind us of the story of Jonah. That reluctant prophet didn't want to do what God commanded because he was certain God would go soft on the very people Jonah had been sent to warn about impending judgment and doom.

Three things seem important as we consider the healing of community. The first is that abundant healing of community is possible. By all the usual assumptions of society's habits and patterns, healing should not be possible and forgiveness and reconciliation should be too much of a stretch to be considered realistic. Yet we must believe that, after the ravages of war, peace can be possible. After decades of slavery, sisters and brothers can join hands. Even beyond genocide and ethnic cleansing, community can rise from the ashes of destruction. Despite anger and guilt, and despite hunger for revenge and retaliation, hearts can be cleansed and renewed.

The second thing to note is that David does not dodge responsibility. Healing happens as we take responsibility for hurt caused and wrong turns taken. As we stop making excuses, blaming victims, and countering accusations with other accusations, the hand of the destroying angel is once again stayed.

The third important thing is that there is a moment of grace as life and health again become realities struggling to bloom in desert places. Our call is to name and nurture each emerging sign of community restored. Songs of joy and celebration ring out as the people of God's love walk hand in hand away from the desolations of yesterday. We can also observe how restoring human community tends to move us toward healing the environment as well. And all the trees of the field will clap their hands!

Prayer

God of each new day, help us name our places of complicity with evil. Help us move from places of resignation and defeat. Help us take responsibility for wrongs we have done and to be open to the ways your love can lead us into a new day, where old hostilities are buried and life-giving partnerships are forged. Amen.

Hymns

"I, the Lord of Sea and Sky" (*Voices United* 509)
"We Have This Ministry" (VU 510)
"We Shall Go Out with Hope of Resurrection" (VU 586)

Prayer-in-Action

List from your knowledge of history and your local scene examples of grace overcoming the desire for revenge, and enemies becoming friends.

No More Missing Persons

I will raise up shepherds over them who will shepherd them, and they shall not fear any longer, or be dismayed, nor shall any be missing....

Jeremiah 23:4

The prophet writes in and of a time when kingdom and community have gone wrong in a major way. The political and religious leaders and many of the people have been taken as captives into Babylon. The people have forsaken God and the law and are facing the consequences. Even the temple is reduced to a pile of rubble.

In the midst of disaster, prophets like Jeremiah proclaim a new day and a renewed promise, when the law will be written on people's hearts. The identity of the people will rely on God's faithfulness and the response of a people who choose righteousness and practise justice and compassion. Of much less importance is the temple, the sacrifices, and all familiar religious practices. Thrown into question is all leadership that betrays the call to service. Bad shepherds will lose their authority and place. God will raise up new shepherds whose priorities will be attuned to the will and nature of God. Reading Jeremiah 7 and Ezekiel 34 helps us get a clearer picture of this message and also gives us a broader perspective on why Jesus called himself the Good Shepherd.

An amazing promise is incorporated into the prophet's declaration when he says, "[N]or shall any be missing." It seems that every generation posts its own sad list of the missing. They are the victims of holocaust and ethnic cleansing, the protesters who have stood up to tyranny, the child soldiers of the conflicts that tear countries apart and fragment ancient communities. They are Canada's women and children and First Nations people who disappear along lonely stretches of highway. They are the victims of poverty and disease, homelessness and hunger. They are the disappeared, the nameless, the faceless millions who do not matter enough to be more than a passing blip on a prosperous world's radar screen. They are the powerless whose votes do not need to be counted, feared, or anticipated. Generation after generation they are numbered among the least important of those Jesus refers to as brothers and sisters.

Through the noise of conflicting messages and the lure of today's temptations, another voice must be heard—a voice that whispers a promise to all who might hear, "And none shall be listed as missing."

None.

Prayer

We remember, O God. We remember those we easily forget, those given little place, those who often have no name or value ascribed to them. They are there in our families, our churches, and our communities. They are there at the edges—strangers, foreigners, illegal immigrants, orphans. They are men, women, and children who are disowned or discounted. Let us see them, God. Let us hear their voices. Let us see your face in them and hear your voice in the words they speak and in the silences that separate them from us. Help us to know in our hearts that when we see them, when we hear them, we will know what it is we are to do. Amen.

Hymns

"Will You Come and Follow Me" (*Voices United* 567)
"We Are Pilgrims" (VU 595)
"My Life Flows On" (VU 716)
"O God, You Have Your Servant John" (VU 718)

Prayer-in-Action

This week invite someone to share a meal with you—someone you have not seen as part of your circle, whom you and others might easily overlook or forget.

Didn't Our Hearts Burn within Us?

[H]e is like a refiner's fire....

Malachi 3:2

Malachi announces a scorching judgment. We have all heard preachers and others who clearly delight in proclaiming that God's anger will consume with fire all the wicked people of the world. Unfortunately, it is often the anger of the speaker rather than of a Holy God that is given voice. Too often we hear the spluttering denunciations of those the speaker hates or fears. The words spoken become laced with ancient prejudices and a call to set things right or to find opportunity for revenge or righteous annihilation.

Many times the "sin" denounced is simply the disobedience of entrenched power. Sometimes it is a questioning of dogma, whether that dogma is a matter of religion, politics, economics, or science. Such denunciations have spawned witch hunts and pogroms, crusades and holy wars, inquisitions and trials.

It is easy to miss another thread that runs through Malachi's proclaiming (3:6–7, 4:2), "I the Lord do not change; therefore you, O children of Jacob, have not perished.... Return to me, and I will return to you.... [T]he sun of righteousness shall rise, with healing in its wings." The purpose of the prophet's call is not to delight in a message of punishment or threat—it is to call the people to a new community filled with redemptive energy.

This theme is repeated so many times in the teachings of Jesus. Jesus comes not to condemn the world and its people but to offer them life abundant—life alive with healing energies that draw the estranged back into community and break down the barriers separating people from people.

Love has the ability to refine us, to take from our living those things that separate us from God, creation, and our sisters and brothers. Love is more awesome than anger. We may hang on desperately and defensively to what angers another, even God. Touched by genuine, uncalculating love, we experience a new birthing in the Spirit. This persistent conversion, this new birth, invites us to lay aside attitudes and habits that inhibit our ability to love others and receive the love of others.

The community of abundant healing is created and recreated by the ever-present love of God and by the striving but imperfect love we have for one another and for the life God gives us.

Prayer

God, we are drawn to the refining power of your love for us and for all. As we are accepted, may we accept others. As we are forgiven, help us learn how to forgive. As we experience healing, let us be agents of healing. Amen.

Hymns

"Jesu, Jesu, Fill Us with Your Love" (*Voices United* 593)
"O Christian, Love" (VU 594)
"When Pain of the World" (VU 598)
"Dear Weaver of Our Lives' Design" (VU 623)

Prayer-in-Action

Before this day is over (tomorrow at the latest) share with another person the story of a time in your life when the love of another person brought you some kind of healing. Be sure to talk about the long-term effect that moment has had on your life and what ripples may have moved outward from that moment to touch others.

Week 5

Wonderful Counsellor: Healing Community

Toe Lint

"Lord, are you going to wash my feet?"

John 13:6

I don't know about you, but I take my feet for granted. I depend on them to carry me wherever I may desire, to do as I wish without complaint, and to continue to do so without much maintenance. I think of them more out of guilty neglect than with intention. After all, when summer rolls around I shy away from sandals—which breathe—in favour of running shoes—which hide. What if people saw my poorly trimmed nails, crooked toes, athlete's foot, fallen arches, and warts? No, they are better left in the dark of concealing footwear.

In response, Jesus bends over, unties my running shoes, and washes my feet. He does not shudder with revulsion at the sorry condition of my feet or at the odour. Instead, Jesus dissolves away the packed dirt from my skin, rubbing carefully but skilfully between my toes without commenting on my collected toe lint. With every motion of his hands I worry he will comment, chastising me for failing to care for the wonderful gift of my feet, for the freedom they provide, for the mobility they promise, for the foundation they endow. Instead, Jesus restores their abundant life and assures me of the deepest love in giving of himself.

It seems a simple action, but it is pregnant with meaning. Jesus has given me an abundance of love that invites me into deeper self-giving and more intentional awareness. His own self-giving is not predicated on my perfection. Rather, his love welcomes me, with all my warts and flaws, neglect and self-centredness. The abundance of his love invites me into a new way of living.

No longer do I need to hide, for there is no shame in who I am. There is only openness and freedom, a foundation for transformation. In that transformation I am called to look at others with similar self-giving love— not to tsk-tsk in disgust at what is hidden, but to invite them to the same understanding of abundance through such overwhelming love. Then, as we wash one another's feet, we too in community help create an atmosphere of transformation founded in love that spills into our aching world.

For now, I'm going to buy a pair of sandals.

Prayer

I watch a sea of feet—
    twisted and torn,
    fresh and filed,
    dirty and diseased,
    trimmed and terrific,
    marred and mangled,
    strong and shellacked—
an abundance of feet,
too many to count,
too overwhelming to love,
        and I despair.
Then your hands lead me,
    one pair at a time—washing while witnessing to love—
    giving of your self,
    without condition, without complaint.
Continue to lead me, O Christ,
    into abundance, into transformation, into life.
Amen.

Hymns

"Jesus Christ Is Waiting" (*Voices United* 117)
"Jesus' Hands Were Kind Hands" (VU 570)
"Bathe Me in Your Light" (*More Voices* 82)

Reflection Questions

What dismays or delights you about your own feet? What dismays or delights you about the feet of others? Does that reflect in your encounters with people every day, and if so, how?

Planting Faith

*"Go therefore and make disciples of all nations…
teaching them to obey everything that I have commanded you."*

Matthew 28:19–20

It was 10:30 at night in the Horseshoe Tavern in Toronto, and I was waiting for the alt-rock band Paint to play. Even though it was Saturday night and I had worship the next morning, I had a vested interest—my eldest daughter plays guitar and sings in the band, and I'm a proud papa.

The lead singer, who is also the lead guitar player, sat down next to me, waiting for the band's moment on stage. I turned to him and said, "I really like the words you wrote for the chorus in the song 'Strangers.'" He looked at me curiously, probably wondering what this old man was going on about. The lyrics talk about our scars and how we often tenaciously hang on to them. Is it because those scars tell a story not of disfigurement but of transformation? Are those scars, like the scars Jesus showed the disciples, illustrations of new life, new challenges, and new directions?

We began to talk (well, bar-scene shout, actually), surrounded by Toronto's usual Queen Street West crowd. As an atheist, he was perplexed to discover I found deep theological meaning in the words of a song he wrote about his former drug addictions and about the scars he bore both inside and etched permanently in the tattoos on his arms. The conversational circle widened to include the rest of the band and two others. It was cool, not because I had any great wisdom to impart but because of the seeming incongruity of location and topic.

We have since had a few more conversations about faith and belief, but I don't think I'm out to make a disciple, much less baptize anyone because of any commissioning from Jesus.

And yet…I can't help but wonder. There are so many opportunities for dialogue. If I truly live as a person of faith, how can any conversation be that far from what I believe? Is faith found where it is planted, and if so, are we just the ones who harvest what God has already prepared? The more I think of the words of the band's song—and of our continuing conversations—I am becoming more and more convinced that the seeds are always there. It is when we avoid these opportunities that we miss going into the world as Jesus commanded.

PRAYER

Command, O Christ, is too harsh.
May I call it a suggestion?
May I wait for just the right opportunity and just the perfect moment?
Or do you insist?
Do you call to us out of the crowds, the challenging masses of people?
Do you beckon from the multitude of eyes seeking, yearning for meaning in life?
Do you push from within?
You tell me, "I am with you always, to the end of the age,"
    but it scares me.
Hold my hand and whisper your guidance.
(*silent prayer*)
Thank you. Bless you. Thank you.
Amen.

HYMNS

"Go Forth for God" (*Voices United* 418)

REflECTION QUESTION

What nudging invitation have you felt today, this week, this month?

Coffee for a Tiger

[B]ut everything they owned was held in common.

Acts 4:32

At 2:00 a.m. on a Tuesday night I would drop in to the Burger King for a coffee on my way home. It was open 24/7 and was far enough away from the university that I wouldn't bump into anyone I knew—perfect privacy while I read my book to relax before bed.

He came over right away, dressed in orange and black stripes, his hand out and a studied, innocent look on his face. "Do you got any change for a coffee?" I glanced over his shoulder and spotted a group of kids around the same age, all in their early to mid teens, obviously anxious that his question prove fruitful.

"Sure," I replied, regretfully closing my book, "How many coffees do you need?" The shocked look on his face betrayed his fears, but I laughed quietly and beckoned the others over. They came, although rather carefully and slowly, gathering around in hope. We walked over to the counter and ordered some food along with the coffee, returning to the tables with this new bounty. Thus began a weekly routine every Tuesday night in the wee hours of the morning.

I later learned he answered to the appropriate name Tiger because of his choice of clothing. He was the leader of the group, even though the school—and family—from which he ran away had considered him a loser. They didn't have much, but they had one another. Just like the passage from Acts, they shared everything—although with much arguing and jockeying for advantage—and distributed it as each had need, including their drugs, booze, and cigarettes. It wasn't out of any sense of scriptural warrant but because they were one family, united in their common life, maybe better called their communal life.

It's been 11 years since I last saw them, and I often wonder what happened to them all. It's been almost 2,000 years since this passage from Acts, and I wonder what happened to us.

PRAYER

O God, in the midst of your abundance, what have I become?
I eat every day.
I have clean water to drink.
I have a place to stay, clothing to wear, and books like this one to read.
Scripture is reading me and finding me wanting.
I confess I take too much for granted through an attitude of entitlement.
Open my heart to the scouring wind of your Spirit.
Open my eyes to injustice and inequity.
Open my arms to embrace the stranger.
Open my faith to receive your direction.
(*Silent prayer*)
Open me to your abundant love in communion.
Amen.

HYMNS

"Behold the Face of Christ" (*More Voices* 114)
"Draw the Circle Wide" (MV 145)

REFLECTION QUESTIONS

How does my faith community give of itself? How might I give of myself today?

Waiting Tables

"It is not right that we should neglect the word of God in order to wait on tables."

Acts 6:2

It gets my blood boiling when people put down wait staff. They work hard, and the work they do is essential to making sure the customer is well satisfied. A good server can smooth the waters if the food is subpar, ensuring the customer returns again. They are the front-line staff who can make or break an eatery, often despite the efforts of the rest of the staff. They are also the ones who take the most abuse from customers. Often servers must have the patience of Job. So, when people imply that waiting tables is beneath them, I steam.

In the reading from Acts, the disciples seem to imply there is a hierarchy, something I don't believe Jesus lived. Not only that, but the most vulnerable of the non-Jews—the widows—are being neglected by those very purveyors of "right" relation. The disciples seem to be getting rather full of themselves as the nascent church grows.

As I point my finger at the disciples, I find three others pointing back at me. I am an ordered minister in the United Church. I believe that God has called me to a particular kind of ministry. Does that make me too big for my britches? Am I buying into hierarchy?

Yet, none of us can do it all. Each of us has been given certain gifts, and each of us can best serve in different ways that, together in a community of faith, become a whole. Even Moses had a problem with micro-managing until he heeded the sage advice of his father-in-law, thus recruiting others to take up some of the burden. God blesses us with an abundance of gifts. Why not take advantage of such bounty? Besides, who is to say that one gift is more important than another and that people can fulfill only one role their whole life long? Aren't diversity and inclusion part of our faith journey in following Jesus?

Excuse me for now, though, because I'm cooking at this week's community dinner and need to get the supplies for the meal. Do you want to come? Everyone is welcome, no matter who you are. I'll even let you wait tables. Just don't forget the widows.

Prayer

Spring: full of potential, of promise, of purpose.
Blow through our lives with purpose, O Spirit,
    that your promise of communion may be lived by your gifts within us,
    that our potential may flower through you.
Weave us as one on your divine loom, O God,
    plaiting us into a whole because of our variety,
    finding the right pattern for the colour and texture of our thread,
    designing us to strengthen the fabric—together.
Allow us to perceive when your pattern changes, O Christ,
    that we may be transformed for an abundance of new patterns,
    all created in your heart of self-giving.
Teach us to serve in light of the gifts you bestow.
Amen.

Hymns

"Body, Mind and Spirit" (*More Voices* 153)
"Deep in Our Hearts" (MV 154)

Reflection Questions

What God-given gifts have you used to serve others in the past year? How have you taken up those gifts to serve your community of faith and your world? How have you been served by others, and how did you respond?

BROTHER?

"Brother Saul, regain your sight!"

Acts 22:13

I had heard of him. Who hadn't? He was armed and dangerous: armed with arrest warrants and dangerously inclined to use brutal force. There was no arguing with him because he terrorized our people wherever we tried to hide. I couldn't believe God was asking me to heal him of his blindness. You might as well ask a lion to eat grass or a child to play safely with a viper. Insanity!

Yet there he was, harmless for now in his blindness but full of dire threat, his temple soldiers hovering at an adjacent table. Why me? Why was I to be the one to risk imprisonment and the scorn of my sisters and brothers in the faith? Why was I the sacrificial lamb in this forlorn hope for change, this generous gift of healing welcome? Had this Saul not done enough damage? For what purpose was I called?

In my strongest, most authoritarian voice I commanded his healing. His eyes no longer clouded, he stared at me with the strangest look, drinking in my features, expression, and humble garb. I thought I was doomed, but he looked more like a lost child, and I felt like his parent standing over him like that. I sat, and we talked while his previously sullen soldier escort leaned in to better hear our conversation. The words just came, flowing past my lips as if of their own volition. I told him about Jesus. I told him he was chosen by God to be a witness to all the world, to witness to second chances, to witness that transformation is possible even for the most stubborn. He smiled in chagrin at that.

Suddenly remembering my central task in light of his healing, I commanded him to be baptized, to wash away his sins and welcome Christ into his heart. Later, we talked long into the night, and I was impressed by the depth of his insight and breadth of his knowledge of scripture. Not many days after— empty-handed but full of heart—he returned to Jerusalem.

I heard some weeks later he fled Jerusalem for fear of retribution. Apparently his previous persecution of we Jewish followers of Jesus upset a few folks, and he didn't feel safe. They were rather suspicious of his story of sudden conversion. They tell me he's going to witness to the Gentiles instead. Fat lot of good that will do. What do Gentiles know of the scriptures? Nothing much will likely come of that decision, I'm sure. What a waste of a healing when there's real work to be done!

Prayer

Help me to see, O God:
>to pierce the mists of my prejudices,
>to quell my fears and still my trembling,
>to know your place in the hearts of us all—
>>strangers or friends,
>>younger or older,
>>athletic or sedentary,
>>street smart or formally educated,
>>boastful or humble,
>>hated or loved.

Heal me; hold me; love me;
>teaching me to do the same for others—
>>even when I am afraid.

Amen.

Hymns

"Will You Come and Follow Me" (*Voices United* 567)
"God in the Darkness" (*More Voices* 17)

Reflection Questions

Recall a moment when you felt you were wasting your time. What made it feel like a waste to you? What might that feeling tell you about your priorities?

You've Got to Be Kidding!

*For it has been reported to me by Chloe's people that there are
quarrels among you, my brothers and sisters.*

1 Corinthians 1:11

I'll never forget the presbytery meeting when I was elected the ordered
representative to the United Church camp in our presbytery. Another
member leaned over to me and said, "Great! Maybe now you can change
what they teach at camp so they are less evangelical and more United
Church."

I was horrified. "You've got to be kidding," I thought to myself. Was my role
to legislate "proper" belief? Was there a new liberal orthodoxy to which we
must all now adhere? While I certainly consider myself well to the left of
centre in the theological spectrum, I have often learned more from those
with whom I disagree than from those with whom I agree. Why would I
consider it appropriate to force others to believe a particular way? Like Paul,
I suggest that we are all called to proclaim the good news.

Over time, and as my own children secured staff positions at another United
Church camp, I was asked to lead a session called "What Does the United
Church Believe?" Once given the topic, I admitted aloud that I wouldn't
mind an answer to that question myself. Nevertheless I struggled with how
to address the question during a two-hour training session. I know the
session was intended in part to get the 40 percent of the staff who were
non–United Church to toe the party line—meaning the official United
Church theological and policy positions.

While I started that first session with great fear and trembling, the
conversation quickly evolved into a discussion of theology, the authority
and interpretation of the Bible, and cultural syncretism. It was pretty
heady stuff! What I noticed, however, was that the more the staff delved
into the issues, the less important their divisions seemed. Instead, they
were engaging in a Spirited dialogue—one in which they tried to clearly
express their beliefs while opening themselves to being changed by the

beliefs of others. It was no longer about liberal or evangelical, historical or progressive, right or wrong. It was about exploring what the good news was for them in the here and now, and how it affected their work with one another, with the campers, and with the parents.

We have had five such sessions over the past five years, and most staff still leave with smiles or frowns and with more questions, but they are changed. They have looked at the good news and found the power of diversity within the Body of Christ.

Lectio Divina

In complete confidentiality, with no discussion and allowing participants to pass if they wish, gather with a handful of people. Ask a different person to read 1 Corinthians 1:10–17 aloud each time. The first time, have one minute of silence after the reading and listen for a word, a phrase, or an image that strikes you. Share. The second time, leave three minutes of silence after the reading and listen for how the passage speaks to your life. Share. The final time, leave three to five minutes of silence and listen for how God may be asking you to be, to change, to act, or to not act. Share. At the end of all of this, pray aloud, one by one, for the person on your right.

Hymns

"Teach Me, God, to Wonder" (*Voices United* 299)
"Creator God You Gave Us Life" (*More Voices* 27)

Reflection Questions

What bothers you the most about those in your faith community? What ideas about your faith trouble you the most, and why? How do you deal with conflict of beliefs in your faith community?

The Princess

"See, the home of God is among mortals."

Revelation 21:3

Born in 1905, married to a prince of Egypt at 20, a mother of seven children by the time she was 30, she seemed to have it all—riches, status, privilege, family, and power. During World War II, she lost it all, her children taken hostage and then killed, her husband murdered due to political expediency, her wealth forfeited, and her power stolen. She fled, for seven long years, calling in every favour she could, finally ending up in Canada in the late 1940s as a refugee.

I met her at the former Queen Elizabeth Hospital in Toronto when she was 91. She was so full of arthritis and overcome by attendant pain that it took her over an hour just to get out of bed in the morning. Her face was like a relief map of loss, each crease telling its own story of sorrow, hardship, and death. She retained her mobility by sitting in her wheelchair and pushing it backwards—the only way she could move independently, and she was fiercely independent!

After breakfast each morning she would go to the coffee shop on the main floor. There she would joke with staff and volunteers. With her quiet, gravelly accent, she was the centre of attention, seeming to know everything about everybody. Intrigued, I asked if I could visit her later that day. "Sorry, dearie," she answered, her face lighting up as she smiled, "but I've got my rounds and no time today, but if you're willing to join me, I'll introduce you to a couple of people."

Mystified, I agreed. We left the coffee shop and took the elevator to the fourth floor—her floor. There she introduced me to her routine of "rounds." Every day, seven days a week, she pushed her laborious backwards way to visit every resident on her floor. Most of them were physically confined to their beds. I watched as she would talk with those who couldn't talk for themselves, seeming to understand what their vocalizations meant. I learned as she reached out with her wrinkled brown hands to caress furrowed brows until agitation and loneliness were replaced with comfort and peace. She wiped away tears, calmed mourning, shared in crying, prayed in companionship, and ignored her own pain. In her wake were people made new each day.

Exhausted after the long day, we chatted in her room, where I heard her story. Expecting resignation, anger, or disgust at her current situation, especially in light of what she had lost, I was surprised to see her face light up as if from within. "I was meant for this," she explained, "God shaped me for this new life. It's like I've been reborn. God is good. Life is good. I am blessed."

In her, God was present. In her self-giving, Christ reached out with healing hands. In her grace-filled love, the Spirit burned away the first things, making all things new. I, too, became a new person that day.

Prayer

Centre yourself by finding a comfortable position in which to sit, feet on the floor and eyes closed. Breathe easily, and open your mind to God's presence. As your thoughts whirl around and around, let them drift away like leaves falling from the tree. Watch each one flit away; bid it farewell, giving way to your deepening feeling of God's presence. Once the tree is devoid of leaves, call up images of the people you care about most deeply. Hold them in your mind's eye, and imagine them bathed in the light of Christ, glowing with healthy well-being. Imagine their cares and worries, illnesses and injuries, and hopes and fears transformed. Continue to breathe easily, and feel the soul-deep touch in the centre of God's heart. When you are calm and ready, open your eyes, giving thanks to God.

Hymns

"Holy Spirit, Truth Divine" (*Voices United* 368)
"God, Help Us to Treasure" (*More Voices* 147)

Reflection Questions

How have you been made new this week? How have you helped others become renewed?

Week 6

Maker of All: Healing Creation

Spirit, Creation, and Me

And God said, "Let...."

Genesis 1:6

I was raised in a church family where the Bible and particularly the creation story were understood literally. I remember as a young child thinking to myself (and only myself, because to question God was definitely not allowed), "If it really happened this way, who was there to write this down?" When I held my first-born for the first time, I looked at his tiny, perfect body and said to myself, "No one can tell me this child is full of sin!" a direct contradiction to the notion that we are conceived in and born sinful.

These experiences were part of my inner promptings to later study theology. Imagine my surprise when I discovered that the book we call Genesis contains not one but two creation myths written by two different authors from two different traditions. The second version begins at Genesis 2, verse 4. Compare them yourself.

What has kept me returning again and again to scripture over the years is its ability to help me hear the Spirit speaking through poetry and metaphor. With the Genesis 1 reading, the word "Let" jumped out at me. The United Church Creed reads, "We believe in God: who has created and is creating." How does the Spirit continue to "create" in the world if it is not through us? This text reads as a continuous invitation to help the Spirit bring new life into creation through me.

"[A]nd the Spirit of God was hovering over the waters" (Gen. 1:2 NIV).[4] The Spirit hovers just as much over our minds and hearts, waiting for us to say "yes" to the Spirit's invitation: "Let...." Let new life emerge from what lies in your heart, for the Spirit hovers over the damaged places that humans have now created on Mother Earth. Oil spills that cannot be

---

4. Scripture taken from the Holy Bible, NEW INTERNATIONAL VERSION®. Copyright © 1973, 1978, 1984 International Bible Society. All rights reserved throughout the world. Used by permission of International Bible Society.

---

contained, melting glaciers and ice caps that cannot be replaced, whole groups of people held captive by unwanted force or poverty—is it not time for human beings to let Spirit move in and through us to bring healing to Mother Earth?

Is there a park, tree, or flower near you that causes Spirit to whisper to you, "Let my Spirit move over this place, and through you, bring life"?

Prayer

Spirit,
let me say "yes"
and invite you to hover
over the places of hurt
in the part of creation where I live.
Stay with me long enough
for me to discern faithfully what I can do.
Awaken your potent, life-giving
strength that lies uniquely in me
to heal this part of your creation.
Amen.

Hymn

"Spirit, Spirit of Gentleness" (*Voices United* 375)

Prayer-in-Action

Ask the Spirit to be with you as you write and reflect about one aspect of creation that needs healing. Ask for guidance on how the Spirit might be calling you to help do this.

Major Cleaner Needed

[A]nd the earth was filled with violence.

Genesis 6:11

The earth was filled with violence because of human beings! Nothing has changed. We continue to live in a world where humans daily inflict violent acts on creation. Countries at war, economic greed, political structures enamoured of power, individuals indifferent to the cries of the earth: our daily news provides a steady diet. Unlike the time when this Genesis text was written, we turn against our very source of life in many ways.

There is a time and place of lament for the "sins of the fathers," which continue to be visited upon generation after generation. We are all connected in one way or another to the violence and to the more minor practices we might not notice, the self-centredness that is ingrained in our daily use of creation. We may feel frustrated and helpless in effecting change over powers that persist in our world. But what power do we have—and possibly grace—to make change in our world, filled as it is with human discord and environmental degradation?

As hard as it may be, we can ask the Spirit to be with and guide us as we look honestly at our own place in creation. It is always easier to blame others than to take what small steps we can.

In Genesis 6, God plans a major cleaning of the earth to rid it of its violence. Yet God recognizes the good worth preserving and carefully safeguarding all the elements necessary for a re-creation. Walking with the Spirit, we will have all that we need to bring about peace and well-being to creation.

It seems to me we can start with a non-violent approach to ourselves and creation. Only then will the Spirit of health and creativity be liberated to work in the world around us.

Prayer

Powerful and wise Spirit,
help me be honest with myself and you
about the ways I do violence to creation.
Wash these away in the flood waters of your grace.
Amen.

Hymn

"Praise with Joy the World's Creator" (*Voices United* 312)

Prayer-in-Action

Make time today to enjoy the beauty of nature. End your time with a prayer
of gratitude.

Hidden Mystery

"Who endowed the heart with wisdom…?"

Job 38:36 (NIV)[5]

"Who has put wisdom in the inward parts…?" is how the NRSV Bible has translated this particular phrase. In the Bible there is often a footnote stating that the meaning is uncertain. The next phrase, "or gave understanding to the mind" has the same footnote: "Meaning of the Hebrew uncertain." I like this.

This particular verse is surrounded by a description of the Mystery that forms, permeates, and sustains creation. The Divine is described with such grandeur that words such as awe and majesty feel too small. My best response is silence, reverence, and deep humility. Even though the meaning of the original Hebrew is uncertain, it suggests to me that the same Mystery described in the rest of the text also permeates us. You are part of the creation being spoken of here. When did you last take the time to have a look and be aware of the marvellous creation you are?

In this scientific age, we know with our minds much more about how the natural world works than did the authors of these verses. Caught up in our stressful lives, with a scientific understanding of how the world works, our default position may be to dismiss or ignore the Mystery that inspires this poetic passage—that Mystery which continues to sustain and permeate all of creation.

Can we allow our hearts to be broken open to the majesty and awe of creation? Can we feel in our physical bodies, imperfect as they are, the mystery of their creation? What do we see when we walk about the earth? Walking the streets of the city, it is easy to see what is unattractive or needs to be fixed. But what natural beauty is there also? In the country, it

---

5. Scripture taken from the Holy Bible, NEW INTERNATIONAL VERSION®. Copyright © 1973, 1978, 1984 International Bible Society. All rights reserved throughout the world. Used by permission of International Bible Society.

can be easy to see the beauty that is there, but we may only see business opportunities, environmental degradation, and loss. What is your point of view?

Prayer

Awesome One,
Father of the Rain,
Mother of the Ice,
Binder of Pleiades,
Looser of Constellations,
Being of Mystery,
Giver of Life,
in this day,
endow my heart and mind
with wisdom that is of you.
Amen.

Hymn

"This Is God's Wondrous World" (*Voices United* 296)

Prayer-in-Action

Take a walk outside, and look long and hard enough at anything you see in your landscape until you experience the wonder and awe evident in this tiny segment of creation. Alternatively, sit silently, breathe into your physical body, and simply feel the sensation of the wondrous creation that you are.

Maker of Scarcity?

You visit the earth and water it, you greatly enrich it.

Psalm 65:9

Years ago I was at a panel discussion. I have forgotten the topic and who was on the panel, but one memory remains. One of the speakers was an economist. He began his comments by instructing us that the first principle of economics is the notion of scarcity; in other words, economics compares our wants and needs with our means, and the results of the choices we make.

In contrast, I had recently reviewed some notes I had taken at a talk given by the late pastoral theologian Henri Nouwen. In his remarks, Nouwen spoke of the abundance of God's love, using as a metaphor the abundance we see in creation. As an example, he described the countless number of seeds that are produced by one maple tree each year, each tree producing enough to create a forest.

Since that time, I have often been acutely aware of the contrast between our culture's belief and our activities based on the economist's emphasis on scarcity. Witness the obvious abundance in nature clearly present in the bounty of crops, hills clothed in wildflowers, seedpods falling from my wisteria, and vast overproduction of seed by other trees, shrubs, and I hesitate to mention everyone's favourite, dandelions!

The writer of today's psalm is suggesting that the overflowing abundance in creation is characteristic of the Creator (the author is obviously not an economist). God gives, forgives, and loves so abundantly that we can say with the psalmist, "We shall be satisfied with the goodness of your house, your holy temple" (verse 4).

As we go about our lives, mechanized, fast-paced, often at a relentless pace, trying to outrun scarcity, the holy temple that is Mother Earth demonstrates the reckless abundance and relentless love of the Creator. May we stop on this day and every day long enough to feel the holiness of the earth of which we are but one part. It is the holiness that supports our feet and, indeed, all creation. May we see and feel the abundance that surrounds us and lies within us.

Prayer

For the abundance of seedpods,
the flowering grain,
the life-giving sun,
the abundance of rain,
I, too, showered by this gift of plenty,
gratefully, I remember.
Amen.

Hymn

"For the Beauty of the Earth" (*Voices United* 226)

Prayer-in-Action

Where is there abundance in your life that you have failed to notice, perhaps in yourself, relationships, or the natural world around you? Take time to notice and write your own prayer of gratitude.

Pulsating Love

[T]he earth is satisfied by the fruit of his work.

Psalm 104:13 (NIV)[6]

It is too many years since I have done it: reclined on a rock in northern Ontario on a completely clear night and gazed at the night sky devoid of artificial light. Each time is like the first, a profound spiritual experience, a truly awe-filled moment. I am rendered speechless (and for me that says a lot!) as deep in my bones I sense incredible grandeur and majesty—there all the time, but rarely seen.

Last year I had a picture taken of my iris to make travel easier outside the country. When I look at my iris, it looks like the ones looking out at me from the eyes of many in my family. Yet when I look into a machine in an airport, it recognizes my iris from any other in the world. I find this completely astounding. How utterly intricate is God's creation, including every part of our being!

Both of the above experiences seem minuscule alongside the ongoing work of the creative Life Force that pulsates continuously through the universe. Words cannot contain what we name Spirit, God, or Creator. Pause for a moment and simply breathe into the creation that you are in your corner of the universe; breathe in your little bit of this energy beyond naming or containing.

In the NRSV Bible, verse 13 reads: "The earth is satisfied *with* the fruit of *your* work." I have rewritten this line to read: "I am satisfied by the fruit of your work." These words reflect my delight in the Spirit-filled creation surrounding me. A question emerges: Can my spirit really say these words to God? Am I really awed by the natural creation of which I am one tiny part? How do I reveal that awe?

---

6. Scripture taken from the Holy Bible, NEW INTERNATIONAL VERSION®. Copyright © 1973, 1978, 1984 International Bible Society. All rights reserved throughout the world. Used by permission of International Bible Society.

PRAYER

May I quiet the outer noise long enough to listen with my heart.
May I quiet the noise of my mind to hear the joy of creation around me
and pulsating through me.
May I find the deep silence within
that allows me to know creation's Mystery
and to find it at home in my heart.
Amen.

HYMN

"Many and Great, O God, Are Your Works" (*Voices United* 308)

PRAYER-IN-ACTION

Open your window, go into your garden, or walk in a park. Listen for the
many sounds of creation. Can you hear their diversity? Gaze at one tree,
flower, insect, or rock. Can you imagine how many parts, cells, and atoms
make up that one natural object? Savour your awe. Nurture it reverently
and thankfully.

O Me of Little Faith

O me of little faith!

Based on Matthew 6:30

If there is a worry gene, I inherited it. But what I and others worry about these days is different from what concerned first-century Christians. Yet, like them, we worry about basic needs for food, clothing, shelter, love, and hope. Increasingly, God's creation is our rightful focus of concern.

Can ancient images really have anything to say to our life, which is but one small strand in the vast web of creation?

The birds of the air and lilies of the fields have simpler lives: "Your heavenly Father-Mother feeds them. Are you not of more value than they?" (Mt. 6:26, paraphrased). What are we to conclude about this scripture? "Don't worry, be happy"? Is this an adequate faith? How are we more valued by God than the eagle circling over the crystal-clear northern lake or the huge coast redwood sequoia swaying in the storm?

When my father was taken to hospital for what turned out to be the last two weeks of his life, I spent the last week of my vacation at his bedside. As he showed signs of improving, my mind turned to the sermon I had to prepare for the following Sunday. I opened my father's Bible to the text. There was a small piece of paper with notes he had taken from a sermon in February 1974. The sermon was on worry, and those words written over 30 years earlier felt like a message to me from God. The final points in the sermon were about the importance of (1) living one day at a time and (2) living each day with God through constant prayer.

And there it is. To step off the worry treadmill, we bring all of who we are—our anxieties and our gratitude—each day, one at a time, to God in prayer. This way, we tap into the nourishing place where the flower's roots stretch out so the blossom and leaves can open to face the sun. Day by day, we anchor ourselves in God, the Divine Healer, and enable that healing power to flow through us to the sparrows and chickadees we joyfully feed and to the lilies we water so caringly. And we discover in doing so that we are indeed cared for and can care for creation.

Prayer

Help me to see the worries in my life that are of my own making.
Let me look to the birds and lilies for simple trust:
that I will have enough,
that I am enough,
that you are enough.
Amen.

Hymn

"Be Thou My Vision" (*Voices United* 642)

Prayer-in-Action

Try writing your own prayer seeking the One who "clothes the grass of the field" (Mt. 6:30) to also surround you with the comfort and wisdom you need to heal and to help heal.

Ultimate Fruit of Creation: Love

"I am the true vine, and God is the vinegrower.
God removes every branch in me that bears no fruit."

John 15:1–2

Pruning is one of my favourite gardening activities. I get a sense of satisfaction from shaping a shrub, tree, or vine and encouraging growth where I want it to occur. We are at the beginning of our growth season after a long period of dormancy. While only a casual gardener, I do know that careful and complete pruning is necessary to produce fruit. So is the tree's period of dormancy.

Being pruned myself by the hand of the Divine Gardener is another matter. The metaphor for the Divine as both the one who prunes the branches and the one who is pruned—the vine—offers many ways of going deeper into the Divine Mystery.

The metaphor takes us beyond our individual garden into the larger garden known as Mother Earth. That is the one and only garden that feeds, sustains, and heals us. Human understanding of the Genesis instruction (1:28) to "subdue" the earth and every living thing has created a poorly maintained vineyard for sustained life. A major pruning is necessary to reign in the weeds and suckers that are choking the very life out of this garden.

The growing environmental awareness around the world is an opportunity for the Divine Gardener to do the necessary pruning through us to balance and strengthen the earth so it can flourish as God's garden. The text in John 15:1–9 suggests that the fruit of a life shaped by and lived in the Divine is love. Not only does the very life of my individual vine pulsate with Divine sap, it depends on that sap for new life and growth. And, including the periods of apparent death and dormancy, the Divine Gardener is carefully continuing to shape me so the fruit of all my life, labour, and growth will be love.

Will we human beings love God's creation enough, including the smaller pieces entrusted to us as individuals? "Abide in me as I abide in you," John 15:4 reads. This love is already in me! "[A]bide in my love" (verse 9). This is my task and challenge! "[A]part from me you can do nothing" (verse 5). In the end I am being pruned for love—abiding in and giving of love.

Sounds so simple—yet it is the task of a lifetime.

Prayer

Divine Gardener,
let me trust you
with the oversight of my growth,
with the pruning I need,
with the encouragement of your water, warmth, and wisdom.
May the fruit of your love blossom in my life
and help to feed our hungry world.
Amen.

Hymn

"For the Fruit of All Creation" (*Voices United* 227)

Prayer-in-Action

Imagine for a moment a beautiful earth with greens and blues, high peaks and deep valleys, wheat growing in fields, gentle breezes, capable of supporting life for thousands of generations to come. What small step in your own life can you take to make this image happen? Remember: pruning begins one clip at a time.

Holy Week

Heart of the Universe: Healing All

Be Still but Awake

"Could you not keep awake one hour?"

Mark 14:37

I once joined a yoga class to heal my back, which had been bothering me since an accident many years before. Among the many positions to learn, one of the hardest for me was sitting still on the floor. The challenge was not just about sitting on the floor for an hour. It was about keeping awake during the time of KwanSang, which means seeing your mind and thought, a yoga version of prayer.

We can see this challenge facing Peter, James, and John as they try to stay awake with Jesus. While Jesus is disappointed with them for their failure to do so, we sense that it is because of Jesus' need for accompaniment. One may recall that Jesus asked these same three disciples to come along with him when he restored Jairus' daughter to life (Mk. 5:37). Once again, he seemed to need to be accompanied in his healing ministry. We can imagine how distressing and anguished Jesus would have been as death approached. In spite of his faith in God, who would save him from death and bring him to life again, Jesus obviously struggled with feeling abandoned.

While I was getting better at yoga in my class, it was still a challenge to stay awake for KwanSang prayer. I am comforted by the fact that I was not alone in this. So many friends in yoga class also struggled. Peter, James, and John, the closest disciples of Jesus, also did. In the midst of this acknowledgement of our failings, we are awakened by one another. Jesus already knew they might fall asleep again, but he needed a community to watch and accompany him in prayer. So we are, in this final week of our Lenten journey, invited to accompany him in joining in the difficult prayer discipline of being still and silent, a corporate prayer for awakening our souls in the communion of the life, death, and resurrection of Jesus Christ.

Prayer

Help us, Holy One,
to be still,
silent before you,
yet awake.
Help us with sitting in silence and staying awake.
Help us encourage one another to accompany Jesus
through the death that leads to abundant healing.
In Jesus' name we pray.
Amen.

Hymns

"O God, Why Are You Silent?" (*More Voices* 73)
"Be Still and Know" (MV 77)

Reflection Questions

Why is being still so difficult? In what ways might my faith community help
me on this journey?

Fire Will Not Burn Us Out

"Do you think that I have come to bring peace to the earth?"

Luke 12:51

"I am not that concerned about our church getting small. The early Christian churches were never big. My concern is that we seem to lose sight of Christian identity and vocation when our churches function in survival mode for the sake of keeping the church rather than discerning what we are called to live, do, and be as Christians."

These are some of the comments from discussions we had in my classes on Christian worship and Christian education. I am impressed and encouraged by my students, who are being trained for ordered ministry—they are neither worried about the shrinking of the churches down the road nor afraid to face the challenges ahead in their ministry.

In today's passage, Jesus confirms the predictions that challenges await. Conflicts and divisions are inevitable, once we understand the meaning of peace, *shalom*, fully and faithfully. Jesus is aware of the consequences of bringing *shalom*—the brunt of its opposition and the suffering to follow.

Facing difficulties is a part of life. Our life is dynamic in that there is constant motion and constant change. Like the moon, the cycle of our faith journey waxes and wanes. Like the fire, the call to Christian leadership sparkles and is blown out. Like a tree, the commitment to Christian discipleship digs in and is uprooted. In the midst of all these changes and movements, our bodies as individuals and as communities wear out and our souls become distressed. However, we are comforted by Jesus' uncomfortable message that there is a reconciliation, like the action of a fire being rekindled (Lk. 12:49).

Lent is a journey of discerning who and whose we are. Such discernment can make our soul soar. Such discernment may also burn a community into ashes. But such discernment will not burn God's people out. Instead, it sustains and nurtures our life into new joy, health, and wholeness. It is like lightning that sets an old forest on fire and births abundant new flora and fauna for all.

Prayer

God of birthing waters and destroying fires,
of waters that frighten and fires that heal.
You bring both lasting inner calm and deep inner challenge,
for you are our identity and our vocation.
Bless us with insight, we pray.
Amen.

Hymn

"God of Grace and God of Glory" (*Voices United* 686)

Reflection Question

Can you think of an experience you have had of division and conflict that led to renewal and health?

Reading the Signs

"You know how to interpret the appearance of earth and sky, but why do you not know how to interpret the present time?"

Luke 12:56

Among many wonderful things about living on the prairies in Saskatoon is the sky. Watching the sky can be lots of fun. This is particularly true for our son Noah, who, like many young boys, has always been fascinated with storms. In spite of his fear of their cloudy darkness, he loves watching storms. But Noah has never seen storms coming as clearly and from as far away as he does in the prairie sky.

While pondering Luke 12:54–56, I understand why Noah loves watching storms. It is empowering for him to sense this incredible natural phenomenon, to see and experience it close at hand. He becomes excited with his own ability to read the signs. That observation of unfolding conditions captures his imagination to the point that he even lets go of his fear of darkness.

Jesus alerts us to attend to the present time, *kairos*, the signs of the Reign of God at hand, the nearing of the end. The failure to read such signs leads to the disempowerment of our own lives. To neglect to pay attention to God's creation, for example, results in the depreciation and even the exploitation of our creation, the creation upon which our lives depend. Our lives are at stake!

There was a record-breaking flood at Fishing Lake, Saskatchewan, in 2007. The cottages near the lake were damaged. To avoid a future calamity, there was great pressure from the cottagers to dig a drainage channel. The Fishing Lake First Nations opposed this proposal because it would endanger the fish stocks and destroy their community. They argued instead that berms be built around the cottages and counselled that there was no rush, that the same bad weather was not going to happen the following summer. The engineers and government officials wanted to know how the First Nations community could be so sure there would be no flood the next year. "Wasps and bees are building their nests and hives low to the ground," said the chiefs and elders. Their wisdom and ability to read the signs and attend to creation were heard. No channel was dug. Berms were not needed. For there was no flood the next year.

Prayer

God of the whole creation,
    You have granted us the wisdom
    to read signs.
    Yet we come before you
    acknowledging that we have neglected to attend to this wisdom.
    Help us to regain this wisdom
    as we learn from children's curiosity and awe before your creation.
Guide us, in this Holy Week, to turn to you,
    as many of our First Nations sisters and brothers do,
    and learn to read your signs.
Amen.

Hymn

"Joyful Is the Dark" (*Voices United* 284)

Reflection Questions

There are many different kinds of signs: natural (clouds darkening), biological (head throbbing), emotional (a smile on a face), social (long applause after a concert), political (who is elected or not), economic (businesses closing), and so on. What signs will or did I see today? Respond to? Prefer to ignore?

The Spirit of Discernment

"The one who enters by the gate is the shepherd of the sheep."

John 10:2

While the Gospel of John contains the loftiest descriptions of Jesus as the Christ, the Way, the Logos, and the Divine, it also paints the most down-to-earth images of Jesus, portraying him with intimacy in close relationships with his friends and others.

The image of Jesus as shepherd is nothing new or striking. What is new and striking, however, is the relationship of the shepherd and the sheep in John 10:1–5. Jesus' identity as shepherd and his leadership of the flock are determined not by outside authority but by the community of the sheep and their ability to discern their leader. Jesus as the Christ is identified by whom he is in relationship with. His identity is affirmed by the group's discernment and response to the shepherd's calling. His leadership is proven by the group's willingness to follow him rather than a stranger.

The sensory experience of hearing reveals who Jesus is just as much as the tactile and kinesthetic experience of knowing and following him. His calling, naming, and leading are juxtaposed by the respectful hearing, responding, and following of the sheep. It is a mutual relationship, inseparable and intertwining.

Sheep can discern their shepherd's voice whenever he or she calls them out of the community flock. Similarly, a mother's hearing can pick up the cry of her baby. Without seeing her baby, or in the midst of many babies' noises, the mother is able to discern which cry belongs to her child. In the same way, I am fascinated by the baby's ability to find his or her mother's voice among the noises of a crowd. This is true for human beings and for countless mothers and babies in the natural world.

Honing our ability to hear God is important in discerning our call. The following is a meditation written and used by my partner, David Kim-Cragg, minister at Grosvenor Park United Church in Saskatoon. Close your eyes and listen for the sounds in this meditation.

We are standing beside a stream. The water is clear, fed by the melting snow. Its shallow current chirps and gurgles over a bed of rocks. We bend down and scoop up a rock from the stream. As we dig our hands into the fast-moving waters, the cold numbs them and makes them ache. We clutch a stone and bring it to the surface, fingers dripping and cold. The stone glistens. It is a stone from the stream of our lives. As we touch it, we discern that it has the shape of fear. It is a fear that has shaped our lives in some painful ways. It is a fear of growth. Fear of change. Fear of others. Fear of being different.

Now we release the stone, and it plunges back into the frigid current, splashing our shoes and legs, disappearing below the ripples of the surface. As we watch all signs of it disappear, we are reminded that the fear of our lives is surrounded by the moving waters of the Spirit. As we let the Spirit move within us and listen for God's voice, the stones in our lives disappear beneath the surface of God's embrace, gently eroding into a new shape, transforming.

Hymn

"Open Your Ears, O Faithful People" (*Voices United* 272)

Reflection Questions

What sounds did you hear in the meditation? How might you listen more deeply to life around you and within you so that you can help to heal the world?

Modelling Jesus' Love

*"So if I, your Lord and Teacher, have washed your feet,
you also ought to wash one another's feet."*

John 13:14

We are approaching Good Friday, the day of Jesus' death. How does his death relate to love, today's central theme?

The story of Jesus' foot-washing is a hallmark of discipleship. This servanthood ritual is only found in the Gospel of John. Maundy comes from the Latin *mandatum*, which means "mandate" or "commandment." The meaning of Jesus' commandment is fully understood in today's passage to wash one another's feet. The coming death of Jesus is not a sacrifice (though interpreted this way for hundreds of years). Facing danger and accepting death are not about denying life or about overcoming human sin. Rather, Jesus' act of departure is an act of love driven by grace, a call to live out his life and identity fully. Jesus gives away his life rather than gives up his life.

To love one another is to live the life of faith fully, even if that life leads to danger and difficulty as it did for Jesus. This refocuses the significance of the cross on what it means for people rather than on what it means for God.

Jesus' death is not in vain as long as his disciples embody his commandment to love. The commandment of loving others as yourself, the ancient Jewish teaching, is seen with fresh eyes when it focuses on love within, among, and for the faith community. It is a renewed relationship. It is a transformed community. And the community, in turn, renews and transforms the world, out of love for love's sake.

The ritual of foot-washing is an invitation to experience this renewed relationship and transformed community. I am aware that literally exposing one's feet to be washed is not an easy practice for many white Canadians, for whom taking socks and shoes off during worship is uncommon. But why not try it? It can be a grace-filled experience full of intimacy and vulnerability, liberation and humility.

Prayer

We are humbled by Jesus' intimate act of love.
    Help us follow this act as we do it for one another.
    Help us renew ourselves as disciples of Jesus
    as we help our community transform in love and service.
Amen.

Hymn

"Love Us into Fullness" (*More Voices* 81)

Reflection Questions

Foot-washing was a gesture of loving servanthood for Jesus. What loving gestures might/did you show today? Can you think of other practices or rituals that model Jesus' love?

WITHOUT DEATH...

Then Jesus cried again with a loud voice and breathed his last.

Matthew 27:50

Jesus' human nature culminates in this moment of his death. His voice, his breath, and his body, soul, and spirit scream and cry out aloud. This human destiny of Jesus' death echoes with the whole creation when the earth shakes and the rocks also scream out. These are signs of solidarity, exclaiming that the whole of creation is with Jesus in his suffering. These events are also a sign of anticipation that the resurrection is on its way.

Many biblical scholars have explored the meaning of the curtain torn in two in Matthew 27:51 and have suggested that the ripping effectively symbolizes the demolition of the idea that the temple is God's only dwelling place. Instead, it is a sign of the promise of the new beginning where Gentiles (and even a Roman centurion) are invited into God's presence. Note that a centurion is the only witness to the event in Mark's version (Mk. 16:39).

Last year during Lent I watched David Suzuki's TV program *The Nature of Things* on CBC. The episode was about how the ocean began. The ocean, the fundamental source of life for the entire planet, began to form in the midst of great volcanic activity 6 billion years ago. It is mind-boggling to think about how this important event began such a long time ago, but I could barely get my head around the idea that the most fundamental life source, water, is actually linked to massive, destructive, volcanic explosions.

I am enlightened by creation's lesson that out of destruction new life is born. I am grateful to the paradoxical "good" news of Christian faith that without the cross, there is no resurrection.

Prayer

God of compassion and passion,
>We feel Jesus' pain and anguish.
>We are frightened by the crying out of the whole of creation.
>We are confused by the blindness of injustice and suffering.
>Help us stay awake through the night to catch the sight of the Roman centurion.
>Out of our blurry tears may we witness the tearing of the division between death and life.
>Out of our sobs, may we become a song of new life.

Amen.

Hymn

"Tree of Life and Awesome Mystery" (*Voices United* 121)
"Christ, within Us Hidden" (*More Voices* 162)

Reflection Question

How can we hold the paradox of our faith, the cross and the resurrection, without dismissing or emphasizing one over the other?

As a Hen Gathers Her Brood

"How often have I desired to gather your children together as a hen gathers her brood under her wings, and you were not willing!"

Matthew 23:37

It is Holy Saturday. Today marks the day after Jesus was killed. We feel stunned. We feel speechless. We feel lost. But we are left with this powerful saying.

Let us enter it more deeply. The rugged path Jesus is said by tradition to have travelled on Palm Sunday went down the side of one hill and then upwards on the side of the next hill, where Jerusalem sat at the top. As Jesus travelled that path and entered Jerusalem, he would have had ample time to ponder this city deeply. Thus, when he was challenged by temple authorities once inside the city, he replied out of the fullness of his ponderings. He chose to use parables: the parable of the two sons, of the wicked tenants, and of the wedding banquet. This he followed with a series of "Woe to you, scribes and Pharisees" and called them "snakes" and a "brood of vipers." This was a profoundly passionate man!

Filled with burning, righteous anger and pain-filled compassion, we can easily imagine—and indeed hear—his heart break wide open when he pronounced the readings for today, his lament for Jerusalem, and his surprising image of a single small, vulnerable hen and her even more vulnerable little chicks.

However sad and painful it is to hear his cry, today's passage is one of the most compassionate moments in Jesus' life. He used the feminine image of a hen to powerfully disclose his identity as the Christ, divine self-giving Love. This verse reminds me of the story of the Chipko movement in India in the 1970s and early 1980s. "Chipko" in Hindi means "to stick." These mainly rural women in the foothills of the Himalayas protested deforestation by hugging and surrounding the trees. From 1973 to 1982, groups of Chipko women braved commercial loggers, developers, and the police, putting their lives on the line to stop the killing of the trees and save the ecosystem they depended on for their livelihood.

As the Chipko women used their bodies to save the trees and the mother hen protects her brood, Jesus dedicated his whole life for us and for the world.

Prayer

Blessed is the one who comes in the name of Lord!
We give you thanks for this experience of being stunned and speechless.
We give thanks for the story of the Chipko women.
Help us to have courage to face the threat of death as Jesus did.
Guide us to walk the way of life Jesus showed us.
Move us to embody your self-giving love
so that we can be renewed as Easter people.
We pray in the name of the Christ who will again be the Risen One.
Amen.

Hymn

"We Cannot Own the Sunlit Sky" (*More Voices* 143)

Reflection Question

In what ways might my personal and communal lives reflect more deeply self-giving love?

Risen to Full Life

"I am the good shepherd. I know my own and my own know me...."

John 10:14

Happy Easter! Day of resurrection! Day of abundant new life!

The apostles found it very difficult to understand what happened that first Easter Day. Do you? From a cold and silent corpse lying in a dark tomb to a radiant, conversing, resurrection body standing in a garden: how can anyone understand such a wondrous change?

Perhaps it helps to think of Easter as a brief glimpse into the fullness of life our human living is a part of, a glimpse of time and space as an amazing web with many strands. The Easter Christ is the centre, holding us together and nurturing us. Each of us is a strand strong in and of itself yet entirely dependent on all the others for that strength. A spider's web glistening with dew drops sways gently in the breeze. Carrying water is hard work—ask any hiker! Yet the web continues to suspend itself, holding the droplets, a minute rainbow reflected in each one. Such strength and beauty lies too in God's beautiful web of life.

Like any web, our Christian discipleship glistens with the interconnection, relationship, and interdependency we have with Christ. It is here that the image of Jesus as shepherd becomes so important to us. Sheep do not follow the shepherd unless they sense the shepherd's genuine care for them, and in this way, the shepherd and sheep develop a kind of language of their own based on that mutual relationship. It is out of their trust of the shepherd—not out of blind obedience—that the sheep want to be with him. They know they are safe with him. This keeps them from going astray: love always leads to life.

We felt stunned and speechless at the loss of Jesus when he died. We are stunned and speechless at the resurrection of Jesus, and rightly so. Our Lenten journey, contemplating the healing of soul, community, and creation, has been a process toward restoring our wholeness so that all life may be abundant.

I end this devotional with an invitation: Find a spider web. Study how each strand is connected to the others. Gently drop or spray a little water onto the web (after asking permission of and giving thanks to the spider). Ponder its beauty and strength.

Hymns

"Dear Weaver of Our Lives' Design" (*Voices United* 623)
"Draw the Circle Wide" (*More Voices* 145)

Reflection

Take a moment to celebrate your sense of relationship with the Easter Christ.

Study Guide

This guide offers five sessions that could be the basis of a one- or two-day retreat or a five-week study. Ideally, participants will have read the devotions for a particular week before coming to a session, but it will not be a problem if they haven't.

Guidelines for Weekly Gatherings

1. Welcome participants as they arrive. Cover "comfort" issues (bathrooms, confidentiality, etc.), especially if some participants are unfamiliar with the meeting place. You might offer refreshments during this welcoming time.

2. Invite all to join in an open circle of chairs around a focus table.

3. When you are ready to begin, light an unscented community candle placed on the table. You might read the following statement at the beginning of each session:

   "Let us invite the Spirit of God to be with us as we gather. We look around us, acknowledging one another, aware that any one of the people we share this time and space with may be the one through whom the Spirit speaks to all of us, some of us, or one of us today. The Spirit of God may speak to and through the heart and mind of any of us. May we be open to one another and to God's gracious Spirit of Life."

4. Invite people to share, as they are ready and if they choose, a brief thought, reflection, particular sentence, or idea that spoke to them as they read and prayed during the past week. This is not an invitation to discuss but an opportunity to honour one another's time of reading and personal meditation. Some may mention an event during the week that brought to mind a passage read or an idea considered.

5. Don't be afraid of pauses and silences.

6. At this point, move into the topic, story, and discussion questions provided for each week/session.

7. Suggestions are made in italics throughout this guide, particularly in Session 1. Feel free to adapt the suggestions to your group's comfort level, style, and wishes.

Session 1
Soul, Community, and Creation

This first session is intended to follow the first Sunday of Lent. Invite discussion and questions about the Week 1 readings if you wish.

Topic

In this opening session, take some time with your group to consider how interwoven is the healing of soul, community, and creation. Health of soul moves us into relationships (community). The community and each person are dependent on creation. Once we start looking, we find numerous places in scripture and in our tradition where attention to one of these aspects soon calls us to give attention to the other two.

This session looks at the theme of healing soul, community, and creation as a seamless garment, and we consider the challenge God's grace brings to our desires and thoughts.

Story

(Read the following aloud:)

I enjoy weaving, and a weaving image comes quickly to mind when I think of the necessity of balancing the health of soul, community, and creation. As I warp my loom I must carefully see that each thread is tied and placed in the correct order through the heddles and the reed. The threads must all be tied with even tension, or the final product will be twisted. The colours in both warp and weft must produce a pleasant design. Each thread, while seemingly insignificant, can either mar the whole piece or fit in and add to the beauty.

So it is with each of us. Our health—physical, mental, and spiritual—has an effect on the way the communities we live in function, and our communities have either a positive or a negative effect on the whole of creation. My prayer is that God will give us the grace to live in love in small ways that will eventually affect our communities and our world with life-giving intention and purpose.

Healing soul, community, and creation depends entirely on our desires and thoughts, yet our call is to think about and live out grace.

Discussion

Reread Eli's story (page 16) and Numbers 12:10–15 (part of Miriam's story, page 20).

- What do you see/hear in each of these stories?
- Is there anything that connects them for you?
- How do Eli's friends view him—as criminal or as hero?

(*Ask each person to take a turn sharing what catches his or her attention in this focus material. It may be an anecdote or remembrance, a question, or a statement that indicates concern or misgiving. Again, use this as a sharing time. Discussion will follow, but at this point it is important that each person engages with the friends who have gathered and with the theme for the gathering.*)

- Where is the wider community in the world of Eli and his friends?
- Who supports them in their daily struggle to survive?
- What do we actually know of the struggles of young people in tough neighbourhoods?
- How can society (we) reach out to them?
- Where and what are the barriers? Within us? Within them? Within our society?

North American society has in recent years seen a greater emphasis on harsher penalties and longer sentences for crime. How does the louder cry to retributive justice square with the gospel emphasis on forgiveness, grace, and restoration to place within community?

What would retributive justice look like if it was applied to crimes against creation? In the case, for instance, of major oil spills in fragile oceans, who would bear the punishment? What would the call to live by grace imply after such a disaster?

(Lead a discussion of the above. In the exchange of ideas, make sure there are opportunities for people to say, "I see that differently." Having individually engaged in reflection and prayer day by day, the group can now engage in discernment that may move them to a place of change and action.

Following the discussion and a brief period of silence, encourage participants to share something they will be doing in the coming week as a response to this time together and the urging of the Spirit. They may have already made these plans, but the question might be how they will approach that action differently as a result of this time of sharing. What each offers is respected and accepted without comment other than the assurance that all will support one another in their ministries for the week.)

Closing Liturgy

(Place a loaf of bread beside the community candle.)

Prayer

Gracious God, Creator of all life,
we thank you for the wonders all around us:
the miracle and diversity of life in plants and animals
in the air, on land, and in the waters.
We thank you for the miracle and diversity of our human race:
flying in space, diving into ocean depths, strolling in a forest,
finding medical cures, distributing food in city slums and ravaged countries,
giving hugs, cleaning homes, learning in kindergarten,
and worshipping in churches, mosques, temples, and synagogues.
Grant us wisdom and courage in our times together here,
that we may learn to live in ways that bring abundant healing to soul,
community, and creation.
Amen.

Hymns

(You might feel more comfortable reading the hymns aloud rather than singing them.)

"Live into Hope" (*Voices United* 699)
"Hope of Abraham and Sarah" (*More Voices* 148)

Scripture Reading
Genesis 19:15–23

(Allow two minutes of silence for everyone to reflect on the scripture. Depending on people's comfort level with silence, you might extend it to six to eight minutes by the fifth session.)

Prayer
Compassionate God,
we thank you for opportunities to serve.
and for those whose examples of service
inspire and nurture us…
(Participants name people who come to mind.)

Help us to be aware of the needs of others…
(Participants name people who come to mind.)

Give us the courage to act when we sense your call to care—
seeking justice,
practising mercy,
showing respect for your creation.

Amen.

(Take time to remember the commitments to action expressed earlier in the gathering time or details of the upcoming week's readings or next gathering.)

Hymns
"Jesus, Teacher, Brave and Bold" (*Voices United* 605)
"Walk with Me" (VU 649; *you might sing the refrain twice, with participants engaging one another by looking around, including all in the group*)
"Behold the Face of Christ" (*More Voices* 114)
"Go Now in Peace, Guided by the Light" (MV 211)

Session 2
Healing Soul

Topic

Today we look at the theme of healing soul through resiliency. Resiliency is an important aspect of the healing of soul, community, and creation. What are some examples of resiliency?

Discussion

In Monday of Week 3 (page 34), we read about the paralytic man who was encouraged by Jesus to get up and walk.

> [A]s Jesus calls us from our life-situations, especially our paralysis, and asks us to take on a new perspective and orientation, from what seems like an ending comes a new beginning.

- What is your immediate reaction to the story?
- Have you any personal experience of being freed?
- Have you ever felt paralyzed in any way, and known that only God could help you move out of that paralysis?

Story

Florence lived in one of the communities that was part of our pastoral charge. She was left paralyzed on one side of her body after the birth of her twins. Florence lived on a farm and had older children and many responsibilities.

With the assistance of her parents, the older children, her devoted husband, and caring neighbours, she was able to raise her family, look after her home and extensive garden, and do many farm chores. She told me the key to her positive attitude was her strong faith. The first Sunday she was able to attend her small country church after being discharged from hospital, one of the older choir members sang as a solo "God Will Take Care of You." Florence felt that it was a message for her straight from God—and she knew it was true.

As an older woman, Florence continued to use her capabilities in every way possible, and as a member of session, she took on the task of sending cards to children for the first five years after their baptism. She was never known to bemoan her losses, only to use what she had to love and serve God's people.

How have you witnessed God's action in community moving people out of paralysis? Do you know anyone who became freed as they let God into their lives, or remained stuck because they excluded God from their lives?

- Who are your mentors and teachers?
- Do you know anyone who has a resilient faith based on trust in God?
- Why do we have difficulty in accepting limitations?
- What positive experiences can you share that show the acceptance of limitations? What examples come to mind when we speak of resiliency of spirit?
- How can we encourage the use of gifts no matter how insignificant they may seem to someone else?

Closing Liturgy

(*Place a gift box decorated with colourful ribbons beside the community candle.*)

Prayer

Ever-present God, we thank you that we are not alone,
that we live in your world.
Help us to place our pain and problems,
and those of others,
into your hands
so we can be open
to the healing you offer everywhere.
Amen.

Hymns

"Open My Eyes, That I May See" (*Voices United* 371)
"God Weeps" (*More Voices* 78)

Scripture Reading

Luke 5:17–26

(*a time of silence to reflect on the scripture and the discussion*)

Prayer

Gracious God, we praise you because, through all of life, you are there.
Open our hearts and minds to your presence and your healing.

We thank you for examples of resilient faith and service in others,
those who inspire and nurture us…
(*Participants name people who come to mind.*)

Help us to be more aware of the needs of those around us…
(*Participants name people who come to mind.*)

Give us courage to act when we sense your call to care—
seeking justice, practising mercy,
showing respect for your creation.

Amen.

(*a few moments of silence, followed by The Lord's Prayer*)

Hymns

"To Show by Touch and Word" (*Voices United* 427)
"Walk with Me" (VU 649)
"Each Blade of Grass" (*More Voices* 37)
"Go Now in Peace, Guided by the Light" (MV 211)

Session 3
Healing Community

Topic

Today we look at the theme of healing community by honouring uniqueness and diversity, and naming and moving beyond oppressions.

Discussion

In the third Sunday in Lent (page 49), we read:

> Into the very midst of this human desire to control, God breathes new life. Stones are rolled away from tombs of convention and control. In valley after valley of dry bones there is a stirring, a moving, a coming together, and a dancing in a unity created by a free and freeing Spirit that is excitingly new and life-giving.

- How do you respond to the phrase "this human desire to control"?
- Have you ever wanted to exercise control over others?
- Have you experienced others pushing you into a mould of acceptability or conformity?

Story

One of our granddaughters goes to a public school where differently abled children are part of the class. The teachers there have a wonderful attitude of inclusion, and the children all celebrate the special triumphs when someone who doesn't often speak is able to add a word to his or her vocabulary, or when it is discovered that music speaks in a special way to a child whose activities are limited and that child responds with clapping and smiling. They learn as a group ways to arrange activities so everyone can participate in some way, even if it's with an extra set of helping hands.

We are all freed when we don't need to have absolute control:

- When have you experienced frustration because some rule prevented you from doing something?
- When has something happened where your first response has been, "There ought to be a rule preventing this"?
- Is control over others ever appropriate?
- What helps keep control under control?
- How might we encourage diversity without losing integrity?
- How might we practise leadership that nurtures freedom?
- What controls could shut down opportunities for change or new directions?
- When does a demand for change limit seeing the good in the "old" ways?
- How can we put in place appropriate control that does not unnecessarily restrict freedom, spontaneity, or diversity?

Closing Liturgy

(*Place multicoloured strands of wool beside the community candle.*)

Prayer

Creator of diversity, we thank you
for the multicoloured and multi-textured world
we have been born into.
Sounds and sights,
smells and tastes delight us.
Physical touches, emotions, and feelings can enrich us
and enrich our joy at being part of your creation.
May we open our minds and hearts to be the people you intended us to be.
Amen.

Hymns

"God, Who Touches Earth with Beauty" (*Voices United* 310)
"When Hands Reach Out and Fingers Trace" (*More Voices* 136)

Scripture Reading
Genesis 11:1–9

(*a time of silence to reflect on the scripture and the discussion*)

Prayer
Ever-present God, we thank you for those whose faith and service to others
deepens our appreciation for freedom and diversity.
We thank you for those whose prophetic, freeing leadership inspires and
nurtures us.
(*Participants name people who come to mind.*)

Help us to find balance in our choices,
ways to include all and to encourage strong and freeing leadership.
Help us to move beyond excess, greed, and inappropriate control.
May we truly live as children of your love.

Give us the courage to act when the opportunity to serve arises
and when we sense your call to care—
seeking justice and freedom from oppression,
practising mercy,
showing respect for your creation.

Amen.

(*a few moments of silence, followed by The Lord's Prayer*)

Hymns
"God Who Gives to Life Its Goodness" (*Voices United* 260)
"Walk with Me" (VU 649)
"We Cannot Own the Sunlit Sky" (*More Voices* 143)
"Go Now in Peace, Guided by the Light" (MV 211)

Session 4
Healing Community

Topic

Today we look at the theme of healing community, which often includes unexpected challenges as well as unexpected gifts.

Discussion

In Wednesday of Week 5 (page 70) we read:

> Yet, none of us can do it all. Each of us has been given certain gifts, and each of us can best serve in different ways that, together in a community of faith, become a whole. Even Moses had a problem with micro-managing until he heeded the sage advice of his father-in-law, thus recruiting others to take up some of the burden.

- How do you respond to this paragraph?
- Can you recall times when you felt overwhelmed with responsibilities and there were people close by who could have taken part of the load?
- Are there people you recall who surprised themselves or others by taking up a task different from anything they had ever done before?

(*This is a good time to share stories of very young and very old people who have taken on amazing tasks after recognizing a situation that demanded a response.*)

Story

Taking responsibility for the well-being of community is something we learn.

The other day I was talking with two teachers who had just returned from a leadership camping trip with grade six students. They spoke of how some students cope well with being responsible for themselves and their belongings and seem prepared to take responsibility in the group. Other students are at a disadvantage because they are used to having others, often their mothers, do everything for them. One child complained that he could not find his puffer. When asked, "Where did you put it when you packed?" he responded, "I didn't pack. My Mom packed for me."

At the adult level we often find that the pool of volunteers for community activities is constantly shrinking. Community becomes a commodity people buy into, not something they create. Even in the church there is often little real challenge to children, young people, or adults to contribute time and energy to produce something of value or to carry out a program that might effect some change in the community.

Healing fractured communities requires time and energy. Maintaining and building the health of a community is an intentional action.

- Do we expect community to just happen?
- Who chooses the direction a congregation takes in its development?
- How have the ways we develop policies and make plans changed over the past two decades?
- How might we take this discussion further?

Closing Liturgy

(Place a well-filled job jar beside the community candle.)

Prayer

Gracious God, Creator of all life, we thank you for the wonders around us—
the miracle and diversity of life in plants and animals
in the air, on land, and in the waters.
Give us wisdom to live with care in this fragile world,
to treat all life with respect,
and to use gratefully the gifts with which you have endowed us.
Grant us wisdom and courage
to live in ways that lead
to greater health of soul, of community, and of creation.
Amen.

HYMNS

"Touch the Earth Lightly" (*Voices United* 307)
"Spirit, Open My Heart" (*More Voices* 79)

SCRIPTURE READING

Acts 6:1–7

(*a time of silence to reflect on the scripture and the discussion*)

PRAYER

God of surprises,
open us to the opportunities that come our way
and to the gifts we have to respond.

May we use our gifts and abilities
in ways that bring health and healing to our communities
and in ways that leave room for others.
We thank you for those whose faith has led to unexpected actions…
(*Participants name people who come to mind.*)

May we respond generously to the needs of those around us…
(*Participants name people who come to mind.*)

Give us courage to act when we least expect to hear your call.
Amen.

(*a few moments of silence, followed by The Lord's Prayer*)

HYMNS

"We Are Pilgrims" (*Voices United* 595)
"Sisters Let Us Walk Together" (*More Voices* 179)

SESSION 5
HEALING CREATION

Topic

Our focus in this final session is the healing of creation. We look at honouring God, the Divine Gardener, who "has created and is creating," and who is served by our choosing to be a people "living with respect in creation." You might also draw the group's attention to any aspects of Week 7 and Easter Day reflections they can look forward to.

Discussion and Story

In Wednesday of Week 6 (page 86) we read:

> I had recently reviewed some notes I had taken at a talk given by the late pastoral theologian Henri Nouwen. In his remarks, Nouwen spoke of the abundance of God's love, using as a metaphor the abundance we see in creation. As an example, he described the countless number of seeds that are produced by one maple tree each year, each tree producing enough to create a forest.

At a workshop I was privileged to attend a few years ago, there had been a fair amount of complaining about not enough this and not enough that. Finally a diminutive First Nations woman rose and said, "I thank the Creator every day that as long as my brother the squirrel is here, I will never starve." The tone of the group immediately changed.

- How do you respond to these paragraphs?
- When does it seem you respond out of a notion of scarcity?
- When do you respond out of a sense of abundance?
- Where are you challenged in this?

It has sometimes been said that we are all better environmentalists when we are discussing issues and places that do not affect us in any immediate sense. Do you agree with this statement? How do we relate abundance to the reality of non-renewable resources used in amounts far exceeding their supply?

Reflection

In his book *The Art of Passing Over: An Invitation to Living Creatively* (Paulist Press, 1988), Francis Dorff speaks of letting go, letting be, and letting grow. He says that it is useful to separate these three for a time and perhaps even consider them in sequence. But then we realize that each is part of the others; they are energies that flow back and forth. All are essential aspects of life, and all tend to be present in each event in our lives.

We have been looking at the healing of soul, community, and creation. We have spoken of an integration of these three aspects in this Lenten study.

- What have we learned of this interrelatedness?
- How has this study changed us?

(*You might read/recite A New Creed*, Voices United, p. 918.)

Closing Liturgy

(*Place a pair of pruning shears and a bowl of fruit beside the community candle.*)

Prayer

(Voices United, p. 911, adapted)

Loving God,
In you, we find peace and possibility.
In you, we find our place.
In your creation, we find our calling.
May we be faithful to you,
this day and all our days.
Amen.

Hymns

"For the Beauty of the Earth" (*Voices United* 226)
"Called by Earth and Sky" (*More Voices* 135)

Scripture Readings

Psalm 65:9–13
John 15:1–5, 9

(*a time of silence to reflect on the scripture and the discussion*)

Prayer

God of love and generosity,
we thank you for your overwhelming gifts.
Forgive our short-sighted recognition of your many blessings.
Help us to live in this wonderful world with care and joy.
May the love that is showered on us all
be a gift that we are eager to share.
Guide us to care for our earth home,
to live in love,
to cherish the interweaving of all life.

We thank you for those whose examples of abundant faith
have deepened our desire to grow in faith...
(*Participants name people who come to mind.*)
May our faith surprise us with its abundant healing strength and power.
May we reach out to help heal creation, our community, and our soul
when we hear your call to care—
seeking justice,
practising mercy,
showing respect for all.
Amen.

(*a few moments of silence, followed by The Lord's Prayer*)

Hymns

"Walk with Me" (*Voices United* 649)
"I See a New Heaven" (VU 713)
"It's a Song of Praise to the Maker" (*More Voices* 30)
"Go Now in Peace, Guided by the Light" (MV 211)

About the Contributors

Gord Dunbar is the Associate Minister of Port Nelson United Church in Burlington, Ontario. He loves terrible puns, ribald jokes, science fiction, quantum physics, playing basketball, pontificating on subjects he knows little about, singing, alternative rock (especially indie music), eating, diet caffeine-free sodium-free Coke, schmoozing a crowd, and manure-disturbing. His three children, Mandy, Melissa, and Ken, keep him grounded and alive. Imagine his surprise when the Spirit called him into ministry: potter's wheel, indeed!

Joan Farquharson lives in Saltcoats, Saskatchewan, where she is able to exercise her love of colour, design, and fabric as she explores the arts of spinning and weaving. There is time to delight in family, community, and creation as, with husband Walter, she enjoys their lakeside home and gardens, a variety of community involvements, and the opportunity to plan and present Enneagram Explorations with Walter. She is a retired nurse and nursing administrator.

Walter Farquharson lives in Saltcoats, Saskatchewan. Although officially retired, he still leads congregations in worship on average twice a month, takes occasional opportunities to write hymns and other things, and is involved in local municipal government and several community organizations. With Joan he enjoys their family and friends, the amazing world of nature, local theatre, and the work they do with the Enneagram. He is a past Moderator of the United Church and an honoured recipient of the Saskatchewan Order of Merit.

Daniel Hansen experienced a call to ordained ministry after serving for many years as a church musician in southern Ontario and the eastern United States. He studied church music at Westminster Choir College (Princeton, New Jersey) and organ at the University of Toronto and Concordia University (Montreal). A graduate of Emmanuel College, Daniel has a doctorate in theology from Boston University School of Theology, where he focused on sacred music and worship. His dissertation was on the role and identity of the church musician in The United Church of Canada. Active as a United Church minister, church musician, spiritual director, and writer, he continues to work to encourage musicians in the church to be spiritually grounded and music to be understood as ministry. Serving in Ottawa and Montreal Conference, Daniel is the father of two wonderful young boys and lives in the Ottawa Valley along with two miniature long-hair dachshunds, Greta and Dominic—the dastardly duo.

HyeRan Kim-Cragg is a professor of pastoral studies at St. Andrew's College, Saskatoon. She enjoys teaching worship, Christian education, and identity formation. She is committed to postcolonial feminist theory, antiracism, and hybrid-intercultural theology. She is a Korean-Canadian mother of two children and loves singing, cooking, and walking.

Margaret McKechney enjoys life as a writer, gardener, artist, birdwatcher, and poet on the Saskatchewan prairies. She draws images from her life experience as a United Church congregational minister, mother, psychologist, and lover of Earth.

Greer Anne Wenh-In Ng, retired professor of Christian education from Emmanuel College, Victoria University in the University of Toronto, and the Toronto School of Theology, is author of the United Church Lenten resource *Tears and Hallelujahs* (1989 and 2004) and co-editor, with Kim Uyede-Kai, of the Advent resource *Birthing the Promise* (1996). She served on the United Church's Theology and Faith Committee, the Committee for Gender Justice, and the Racial Justice Advisory Committee. She was also interim General Council Minister, Racial Justice, in 2005 and (Toronto) Conference Minister for Social Justice and Ethnic Ministries from 2006 to 2009. Wenh-In continues to practise the presence of God in her time and space by engaging in the embodied disciplines of Taiji-qigong and Chinese brush calligraphy.

The Rev. Dr. Anne Simmonds is an ordained minister in The United Church of Canada and pastoral associate at Metropolitan United Church in Toronto. She is currently adjunct faculty at Emmanuel College, where she teaches courses in death, dying, grieving, and prayer. She lives in Toronto, where she offers spiritual direction and counselling, workshops, and retreats, all of which draw from her experience as a former nurse, hospital chaplain, and congregational minister. Her website is www.annesimmonds.ca.

We'd love to hear what you think of this book.
Please visit www.united-church.ca/sales/ucph for an online feedback form
and an invitation to write a review of this book.